# MOTHERCRY

# MOTHERCRY

Languaging longing and loneliness
through the omphalos
of ageing mothers of adults

A love song for the motherline

Stephanie Dale

First published in Australia in 2026
by Writing for the Brave
ABN 60 889 920 117
www.stephaniedale.com.au

Copyright © Stephanie Dale 2026




National Library of Australia
Dale, Stephanie, 1959–
Mothercry: Languaging longing and loneliness through the omphalos of ageing mothers of adults / Dr Stephanie Dale.
ISBN 978-0-9807043-6-5 (paperback)

A catalogue record for this book is available from the National Library of Australia

Cover design by Stephanie Dale
Celtic mother knot image by Clip Art Library
Typesetting and eBook formatting by Sunset Publishing Services Pty Ltd

Other books by Stephanie Dale

*My Pilgrim's Heart*

*Hymn for the Wounded Man*

*Write Your Way Home*

For Bear Rose, who never left.

For my mother.

I am all she was and more.

The more is to her credit.

# CONTENTS

*Silence like a cancer grows*
*Hear my words that I might teach you*
*Take my arms that I might reach you*
*But my words, like silent raindrops fell*
*And echoed in the wells of silence*
From 'Sounds of Silence', by Paul Simon


*"… the only genuine ideas are the ideas of the shipwrecked."*
José Ortega y Gasset

# ABOUT THIS BOOK

This is a book of experience, ideas and knowledge. It is a brave book, one that asks readers to approach with tender heart. It is the culmination of my research into the modern western contagion of ageing mothers' alienation from their adult children. I found my way to this topic through listening to the ageing mothers who showed up in the countless writing groups I have run over many, many years. Shared in groups, or told to me late at night confidentially after a wine or two, or buried in unpublished memoirs, or disclosed as the reason why a fledgling writer is dithering rather than writing, I came to realise these were not isolated personal experiences but a sinister outcome of changed family dynamics in our times. I saw the pattern, a glut of cancelling and ghosting in the space of two generations. It is a pattern I recognise in my own family.

Burrowed into the conceptual belly of this book is the 'omphalos stone', a motif I have borrowed from the ancient temple of Delphi to represent the elders-with-voice missing from the heart of industrialised western family living. The omphalos stone was a bee-hived shaped rock the size of a small boulder. It was covered with a net-like pattern symbolising the web of life. It represented the cosmic axis, connection point between the heavens, the earth and the underworld, and was a symbol of mystery and guidance. The omphalos stone, says philosopher Peter Kingsley, was "more than a symbol. It was alive. It was the place where worlds touch. A channel. A passage. And those who guarded it knew how to use it". Journeying to and with and beyond the omphalos stone drew me deep into the entangled territories of Longing, Loneliness and Love.

This is a phenomenological project. To write phenomenologically is to surrender consciousness of self and enter the unity of existence. Therefore, the personal accounts of ageing mothers of adults have been presented as direct experience, third person accounts, interview extracts and diary extracts. The form of presentation of each anecdote is dependent entirely upon what the rhythm of the text required. For love of the shipwrecked, I have made every one of these tellings my own. Hence, other than the narrative spine, the first person 'I' accounts in this text are not my own experience. I have made this decision by virtue of common ground, to protect the ageing mothers of adults and their offspring, and for love of surrender to the phenomenological writing process. In the words of Adrienne Rich 'I have come to see the wreck', 'to see the damage that was done and the treasures that prevail'.

Adrienne Rich described the phenomenological process when she came to see:

> *the wreck and not the story of the wreck*
> *the thing itself and not the myth*
> *the drowned face always staring*
> *toward the sun*
> *the evidence of damage*
> *worn by salt and sway into this threadbare beauty.*

*Mothercry* is an expedition, a rite of passage, a reclamation. It is a journey to the threshold of rightful power. Like the little drummer boy who played his drum when there was nothing left to give, it is my offering to the people of Earth, and, by extension, all life forms. This text makes no claim to philosophical or academic grandeur. Rather, it is a cherry picking, a weaving, a standing on the shoulders of the work that has gone before, plucked in elements from grand bodies of work to generate the book I would have liked to have read these past years. It is not commentary on any individual. It is generalised comment on modern western nuclear families and the societies in which we make our lives, told through a sweeping arc of thought, knowledge, ideas and experience.

Throughout this text are the voices of women who are partnered, unpartnered and untethered (belonging to no community). They are women with vast financial resources and women without much by way of financial resources. They are women with grandchildren who are young and women with grandchildren who are grown. These distinctions are important, as this field is so unmapped the women themselves often have scant understanding of the subtle nuances in the experiences of others in seemingly similar circumstances. So too readers, among whom further distinctions include those with children and those without children, those whose children are older than forty and those whose children are young or early adult, those whose grandchildren are young and those whose grandchildren are grown, as well as those in clanned families, matrixes of nuclear families and isolated nuclear families.

These distinctions are the differences between receiving the treasures herein or piling on further dismissal, shaming and/or scorn for the nuanced experiences of ageing mothers of adults, the kinds of experiences psychiatrist Frieda Fromm Reichmann described as 'incommunicable and cannot be shared by empathy'. Frieda's point was made by a dear friend, when we were on our second glass of *rioja* and I risked speaking candidly about this book. In a voice as resonant as the herald throughout the land, she snorted: "I don't believe you." She is a financially secure, partnered woman with no children who counts herself among the socially and politically astute.

That dismissal validated the three years of my life I dedicated to this project.

Immeasurable thanks are due to Patt Gregory, for her friendship and faith in the value of this text to the world; to Mary Maher, who insisted I return to the page when I insisted I was done with this subject; and Susan Moriarty, Clare Finegan, Trish Ganly, Martina

Carroll, Mags Amond, Anna Kimberley and Kathleen Noone. Thank you all for your critical engagement as I finalised this text.

To the ageing mothers of adults who shared their experiences with me, whether through friendship, chance encounter or formal interviews, I am enormously grateful for your courage, your openness and your engagement – *thank you*. This book is testimony to your bravery, and to your genius for living well with the breaking heart.

Still we rise.

# INTRODUCTION

This is a book about ageing. Specifically, it is a book about what it is like to be an ageing mother of adult children in a modern western industrialised family, and economy. I am an ageing mother of adults. I did not see the reality of what this means coming. Decades ago I won a journalism award for representing the voices of older women in the media. I have written and read stories about the loneliness, invisibility, homelessness of ageing women. Still I did not see it coming. I turned from the hurt in my mother's, grandmother's and great grandmother's eyes. And still I did not see it coming. A dear friend and I have long reminded each other that every woman who speaks, speaks for the first time. This is my speaking, and rather than speak for the first time I am speaking through compilations of experience, conversations with friends, remembered conversations among friends and strangers, and formal research interviews with ageing women who are mothers of adult children, which is to say, people they mothered from birth who are older than forty. The accounts I have related were selected for their echoes in the experiences of other ageing mothers of adults, and they have been paraphrased for purposes of assured anonymity. All the accounts are illustrative of the mythmaking that silences the voices and shatters the hearts of ageing mothers and grandmothers of adults.

I am also speaking through the persuasion of a woman whose name you know but, unless you are an ageing woman, whose work you are unlikely to have encountered. Simone de Beauvoir wrote an entire treatise on ageing when she was an ageing woman. If I had read this book when I was younger I might have missed the sharp edge of an ageing woman's tone between the lines. What Simone had to say then is as relevant now, as if she had never written it at all. Almost. With the rise of the giant retirement funds, politicised economics for swathes of the retired working class in western nations such as Australia are altered. The realities of the phenomenology of their living are not. Hence I am heeding Simone's summons to shatter the silence. Again.

There is nothing new between these pages, nothing that has not been spoken, written, experienced, researched or thought before. Yet I speak it again, this time through the amplification of a key finding in my PhD – the imperative of languaging the feeling body through writing to health and wellbeing. Whereas Simone delivered a back story on ageing through the research, writings, arguments and observations of anthropologists, historians, gerontologists and sociologists, this book plucks at the familial, social and cultural landscapes of ageing now, situating the experiences of ageing and elderly mothers of adults inside the modern western industrialised family, and economy.

The economy. Until I entered the disappearing state of the ageing woman, I thought the Cost of Living Index was a theoretical economic measure. I now know it is the contextualised cost of staying alive on this planet. The not-wealthy ageing and elderly will shudder at those words: *cost of living*. One bright, highly competent ageing mother of adults said to me: "I'm just going to have to die." She meant it. She cannot afford the cost of her living. She is preparing a folder. She has a heart ready to explode. Literally, and figuratively. And if you are paying attention you know they are the same thing. An ageing man I know said he planned to hire a beautiful boat and sail into a hurricane. Not because of the cost of living (his gender reveals no surprises there), but the deplorable options for dying on offer in the modern western industrialised family, and economy.

This book recognises three stages of ageing: pre-ageing, ageing and elderly. It is concerned with the middle phase: ageing. Prior to entering the state of ageing, there are moments of notice: the hair greys, the bleeding stops, lines no longer leave the face. At this time in my own life, friends more concerned than I would ask: 'What are you going to do?' Note the unspoken worried whisper, the unfinished clause: 'When you can't afford the rent/run out of money (and so on).' In my fifties (a pre-ageing woman) I would quip 'pitch a tent in a warm place with friends, fish, grow vegetables, light a fire, and laugh like old women about the precarity of our lives'. This prompted two responses: 'Oooo that sounds like fun' and 'Can I come too?' And it did sound like fun. And I'm counting on them coming too. The truth is, in my fifties I failed to comprehend what it is like to live as an ageing woman in an ageing body. I now see, burrowed into the biological heart of both responses, two states of being common to that unhurried class of people known as 'the elderly', men and women – first, that the ageing body is a physically challenging place to live: it is ongoingly painful; and secondly, and primarily given their isolationist natures, longing and loneliness.

I began this project by drawing a speculative thread between loneliness and longing. For what is loneliness if it is not longing – longing for, longing to. And what does acting on our longing ask from us if not immeasurable courage. I know this in two discrete ways: 1. my research shows that acting on behalf of our longing asks more from us than we think we can bear, including confronting old shames and overcoming deeply embedded fears of exposure; and 2. simple really, if acting on longing was easy to do, we'd do it. The fact we'd rather live with the burden of unactioned longing than act upon it says all we need to know. Do we have a 'mental health crisis' or do we have a crisis of longing and loneliness? And no, they are not the same thing.

Thus we return to the worried whisper, 'what am I going to do?', code for the haunted longing to know we are taken care of in our old age, as if responsibility for food, housing, social engagement, health and wellbeing rests entirely on the shoulders of one ageing or elderly woman, or man. Theirs to bear alone, despite and/or regardless of the situational familial, political and economic contexts of their living. That most vicious phrase of our times chimes in: "She made her choices", as if there are no other influences on a woman's life beyond her 'choices'. What the modern world calls 'choices' are in reality countless small daily decisions that lead us to where we are today. For human beings the world over, those apparent 'choices' were never supposed to lead them 'here'.

This book describes what it *feels* like to be an ageing woman in a modern western family, and economy. It chronicles the feelings of outsiders pressed up against the window frames of unscrutinised yet conceptually impenetrable family borders, and the impacts on their bodies as they collide with boundaries and building blocks foundational to family living in our times – conceptualisations we contributed to, constructed and condoned when we counted ourselves among the empowered young, neither ageing nor old.

This book describes what it feels like to live without language that represents our living. It refuses jargon peddled by scientists, experts on career trajectories and policy makers beholden to expedient economics. Their language neither represents nor embraces nor includes the actualities of the beating heart that must live out the programs, paradigms, policies, statistics, strategies, theories and *avant-garde* systemic whims imposed upon our living by the empowered young and middle aged. This book is devoted to returning the language of the living people to the living people.

We are a society that has experienced the simultaneous rise of the spiritual new age and mental health industries. In recent decades these industries have privileged us with the right to judge, loathe and blame our parents and others for transgressions real and imagined, as if our individualised personal experience is the only one that counts; as if one or two human beings, decontextualised from time, place, experience and generational inheritance, about whom and which we know nothing, or very little, as if those individuals are responsible for all the ills and limitations we ascribe to our own lives; failing also to understand that the story we tell about our living is always the story we can bear and the story we can bear changes with the tides and times of our lives. This bitter telling of our lives is far too narrow a bandwidth for healthy individuals and society to grow, let alone thrive. 'Be happy' is a bumper sticker and 'be kind' is an email signature, while all around us the children are neurotic and the elderly want to die. These trite times are demonstrative of what happens to a society without elders-with-voice.

As Simone blandly pointed out, the surprise in the story is that the young do not recognise themselves in the ageing and elderly. Or they do and deny its coming. Certainly they fail to comprehend that what they do will be done to them, that how they treat their parents and grandparents, their elders, *will be* how they are treated when their hair greys, the bleeding stops and skin surrenders to gravity. Intellectually they may know this. Their actions speak otherwise. Buying your mother a nice room in a nursing home won't save you. The denial the ageing themselves perpetuate is not helpful. When I called my mother 'old' she would say 'old*er*', as if an extra syllable changed the reality, although I'm being wilfully blind if I do not recognise what she was trying to say. Other women I know express their denial through such idioms as 'age is just a number' and 'you're only as old as you feel'. The fact is the extra syllable to which my mother clung was her lifeline in a society that had entombed her in the mausoleum of 'wise and kind'.

We know she is 'wise and kind' for no better reason than one glance at her archetypal grey hair, slowish gait on an effortful day and saggy skin tells us so. So too, would we know her as old and snappish should she present as the same person with tight lips and a frown. The point is, it is the body that does the ageing and the body the world fixates upon as it decides whether we are 'productive', or 'beautiful', or 'intelligent', or 'capable', or 'great for her age', or 'past her prime', or 'worthy of genuine interest (not the same as 'get her story for the historical record before she dies')'. It is the body in the world that alters our status, and determines our situatedness in family, community and society. Psychiatrist Thomas Hora may get kudos for pointing out that problems facing individuals are always psychological, and solutions always spiritual. I am left to wonder, however, what about the body? It is the body upon which and in which and through which the dramas of our lives are acted out. It is the body that does the feeling of our lives and it is the body upon which this entire discourse rests.

Humans tell the story we can live with, the story we can bear. With the rise of the spiritual new age and mental health industries these past decades 'stories' have been on the ascendancy. I'm staking a flag in the ground that claims stories have had their day. Not as entertainment, but that is all they are. It is time to face the reality that stories are not true. Stories are myths of our own making. The body, on the other hand, the body remembers. The body knows. Trauma specialist Peter Levine is unequivocal that it is through sensations in the body, not talk therapy, that trauma will be transformed. Insight, he says, does not equate to change. It is the feeling body that holds the trauma, and it is the feeling body that enacts the change.

*Mothercry* goes further. My thesis is that in order to make genuine efforts towards redressing the epidemic of loneliness among children, the ageing and the elderly in modern western industrialised families and economies, it is not only the feeling bodies of the living to which we must turn our attention, it is languaging the feeling body that is our next evolutionary challenge. Before the story, the feeling. What are the words that might speak for a feeling? The actual feeling, before the story kicks in. Until and unless we are willing to hear what living lonely feels like to the body living lonely, all efforts to address the 'mental health crisis' are in vain. It is, after all, the body that does the living, the body that does the feeling.

The foundational word of modern western industrialised living is 'I'. My. Mine. Me. You (not me). The society of the sanctified individual. The individualised self is a blessing for the power years (mid-twenties to mid/late fifties). It's a shitshow for children and the elderly. Every day I send an apology on the wind to a heaven I don't believe in. It is for my mother. "I am sorry." And my grandmother. "I am sorry." And my great-grandmother. "I am sorry." I know I am not the only one. For as we enter the state of ageing, the brutal reality of what has been done to our mothers and grandmothers, individually and collectively, is slugged home. That 'all about you' permission slip of no or minimal responsibility to and for clan has returned to roost. It hurts. It hurts up and down the family line. I am now witness to my own behaviour in the adults I birthed and raised, and in grandchildren born to a daughter not old enough to vote and to whom I devoted my best years. It hurts because I see in my mind's eye my bewilderment reflected in the eyes of my mother, my grandmother and my great grandmother, all of whom I knew. The slow burn exile made apparent through generational eyes. Crudely interpreted those old women may as well be saying WTF? WTFF. *How did it come to this? How did those beautiful babies come to this?*

'This.' A four-letter word that is the point of this book. The 'this'. What is the 'this' we have come to? What words describe 'this'? What does 'this' feel like for the ones living 'this'? I'm sure old men, too, endure the excruciating unanswered longing and loneliness common to old women. I wonder, though, if the exile of ageing comes upon men fast and late, given they sustain their value as humans-of-worth longer than women, and are ascribed greater worth in the world than women throughout their lives.

Harriet Rubin says age is a feminising process for men, so perhaps in the end gender is irrelevant, or relevant only so far as our personal experiences of living have been shaped by the influences, experiences, expectations and impositions of gender during childhood and the ensuing power years. Certainly, given their greater earning capacity and dominion over the world's assets and financial resources, the looming state of ageing must be experienced differently for men as the power years close in, although there will of course be exceptions and those exceptions may be significant in number. It is likely the experiences of ageing and elderly men and grandfathers are mirrored in these pages. Longing and loneliness are human states, after all, independent of biology, gender, wealth and resources. Ageing for women, however, is a slow burn exile, and it is the experiences of women to whom I have given voice, by nature and design.

Ultimately, though, this is a book about all of us. After all, every human in the world has a mother, two-thirds of women will become mothers and almost all of us can expect to reach old age. Through the experiences of ageing mothers in western families and economies, this text plucks longing, loneliness and love from the melee of emotional theory and posits an entirely new frontier for understanding these primal, universally human, forces.

*Mothercry* makes no claims to theoretical depth, oversight or examination. This book seeks not to enter into ideological point scoring, nor to lament the loss of relevance of an ageing woman. This book is a contribution to facing the reality that western industrialised ways of being in the world are not working for us, for any of us. *Mothercry* selectively harvests the ideas of our time, and the ideas that have shaped our times, weaving old ways of being with fresh understandings, offering what physicist Karen Barad described as 'new-old' ways of seeing and being in the western world. It explores the felt realities of the ageing bodies of mothers of adults in a bid to find our collective way through to a liveable solution in which the children (ad)venture outside again and adults do not want to die. This book is my tribute to the voices and experiences of mothers and grandmothers who have lived through, or are living in, modern western industrialised families and economies.

Phenomenologically speaking, through the words and experiences of ageing mothers of adults, we will enter and explore the essence of 'this'. This longing, this loneliness, this love. The 'this', there for all the world see, or, if we dare, feel, in the incomprehension and hurt in our grandmothers' eyes.

# 1.

## Languaging Longing and Loneliness

I AM VISITING Rose. She is old, a wizened American from Ohio at home in a cabin on the edge of a mountain. Rose with her humpback, cackling laugh and crack New York City accent when she wants to be funny. She asks about my kids. She means the adults I birthed and raised who are in their mid-forties.

"I loathe them," I say.

Rose knows a lot about life. When she drops the New York City routine, hers is the voice of the mystic speaking the ineffable. She leans forward, as if to invite a different response. New York City Rose shoves my wicked words back down my throat.

"But not really," she says.

Rose is the second friend in a short space of time to refuse me these unsanctified words. A heated stillness ignites in my bones. I lean forward to meet her, look right into her face, and repeat myself.

"I loathe them."

There is steel in my voice now, that Rose of all people would deny me these words. There is also fortified fury in my body for the ageing mother whose experiences with their adult children mirror mine. Ageing mothers whose voices are silenced. Ageing mothers denied their words. Ageing mothers refused their languaged experiences of family made audible in the world. Ageing mothers who deny their own words for fear they are the only one, *oh the shame, oh the pain.* Ageing mothers who deny their words for fear they are the only one who endures the agony of thousands of small arrows that pierce a woman's heart, but do not kill her. How much can an ageing mother of adults take? So very much. So very much. So very much.

There is one story permitted the ageing mother of adult children and grandchildren, and that is the one that tells the world how fortunate we are to have them, the one that tells us we must be so proud of them, the one that tells the world of our delight in our grandchildren. Oh we're so lucky to have them. So lucky. There was a time I thought so too. Until those tiny arrows brought me down. I refuse to die in this forlorn place alone for no reason other than when I speak just one tiny arrow to an ageing mother whose heart is also spiked with arrows I see the flicker of recognition in her eyes. Occasionally, rarely, I strike wildfire and our shared realities tumble out.

Through a waterfall of unemotional tears I tell Rose of my decade of painful experiences with my adult children and adult grandchildren. I tell her what it feels like to be 'useful, not included'. I tell her that I will say I loathe my adult children until I am allowed to say I loathe my adult children. I tell her I will speak these words until all the ageing mothers of adult children have language and licence to speak their experiences. I tell her my adult children can be simultaneously wonderful in the world and awful to their mother. I tell her my adult children are not special in their awfulness, that the loathing of the ageing mother is a contagion in our society iced over by platitudes and mythmaking and a mental health industry that divides families and empowers the expert-young to guide the troubled-young upon whom their livelihoods depend. I tell her that women's voices and experiences have been claimed and proclaimed in these apparently post-feminist years, yet the voices and experiences of the ageing mothers of adults are disallowed. Why is that? The ageing mother in constant service to her adult children is denied her voice and experience, and into the whistling silence the small arrows fly.

My friend Laura knows what I mean. The realities of our adult children accompanied us on daily walks during the COVID-19 pandemic. One morning I tell her I've decided on my epitaph. She raises her eyebrows in invitation.

"Fuck off," I say.

We could barely keep ourselves upright for laughing. We are still laughing. A weedy headstone among the rows engraved with an ageing mother's final words. An epitaph for the bruised mothers of adult children. In my case, I am the bruised mother of adult children and the bruised grandmother of adult grandchildren. Laura does not envy me two generations of bruising adults. That I would know my grandchildren well into adulthood was once the crowning glory of my life, uncommon in my generation of 'white' western women. One generation of bruising adults and I'd be a heart full of arrows still standing. Two generations brought me down.

## Phenomenologically speaking

Phenomenology is the study of the essence of things. It is the disciplined quest to know the *being-of* the thing, eventually to communicate to others, or attempt to communicate to others, the nature of the phenomena itself. The work of the philosophers, researchers and scholars named in this book can be traced to the realm of phenomenology: Simone de Beauvoir, Hannah Arendt, Frieda Fromm Reichmann, Philip Koch, Karin Dahlberg, Ludwig Binswanger, John McGraw. This book is less concerned with explaining theories than making dedicated effort towards describing the experiences of the enspirited bodies of ageing mothers of adults, her body doing the living in the world. Phenomenology is our portal into and the pathway through those experiences, describing what it *is* to live as an ageing mother of adult children in modern western industrialised families, and economies. By extension, phenomenology is the means for recognising and understanding the essences of longing and loneliness in the feeling human body, with the intention that this will deliver genuine redress for the health and wellbeing crises endemic to modern western living.

This is a book about bodies: ageing women's bodies, pre-ageing adult bodies, corporate bodies, nuclear familied bodies, clanned and unclanned bodies, partnered, unpartnered and untethered bodies. All human doing, being, thinking, feeling and knowing is enacted through the body. Human bodies, need it be said, are not only necessary to human existence they *are* human existence. Bodies are vulnerable to that same existence. Bodies circulate. Bodies communicate. Bodies cry. Bodies speak. Bodies laugh. Bodies break. Bodies think. Bodies remember. Human beings exist through the body and, thus far, only through the body.

Do some bodies matter more than others? Whose bodies matter? In what circumstances do different bodies matter? Are all bodies equally visible? Are the voices of all bodies equally valued? Who decides which bodies matter? Well bodies are functioning bodies, yet how well does a body need to be to function? Who decides? These are neither indulgent nor idle questions for health and wellbeing research, policy and practice which has long revered objectivity as true science and, faithful to objective binaries, has scorned subjective counterparts.

Philosopher Jürgen Habermas referred to this unexamined faith in objectivity as "scientism", which he defined as "science's belief in itself". The historical (not ancient) locus of western human health and wellbeing research, policy and practice has been rooted in the medical and psychological sciences. The medical and psychological sciences' obsession with objectivity has been disrupted in recent decades by the expansion of health and wellbeing research into other disciplines, and of course with the expansion of scientific exploration and discourse into the quantum realms, where that which was unequivocally known begins to dissolve. For the purposes of this book, scientism is that which reduces human bodies, human living and human experiences to statistics, measurements and scales. Philosopher Donna Haraway observed that 'objective' science is by definition disembodied science. Physicist F. David Peat contends that western science is "by no means … objective, neutral and value free", and that technologies considered progress in one world can be catastrophic for bodies residing in other worlds.

Peat argues that the more-than-material science of indigenous knowledge systems that embed human bodies inside webs of relationships enhances the capacity of the dominant western paradigm to address challenging global problems, including individual, family, community and planetary health and wellbeing. Western wellbeing measurement scales and methods skew research results, privileging dominant cultures and demographics and displacing others. They reduce personal experiences of wellbeing to numerical aggregates that either fail to capture or ignore nuanced cultural experiences. Haraway calls this "the privilege of partial perspective". The western wellbeing research industry is rooted in the affluent values' systems of North America. It ignores interpersonal complexities and focuses instead on individuals at a time when the health and wellbeing of individuals, communities and our planet depend upon the mobilisation of *relational* research paradigms.

There are therefore three phenomenologically-adjunct health and wellbeing theories embedded in this text: salutogenesis, dwelling-mobility and wellbeing-as-assembled. Western health and wellbeing research, policy and practice is predominantly pathogenic – its focus is what makes people sick. Salutogenesis is a health and wellbeing paradigm that focuses on what makes people well and keeps people well. Medical sociologist Aaron Antonovsky argued that people are not either well or sick, as per the pathogenic paradigm. Rather, he observed that people can always be found somewhere on an ease/disease continuum, and that this 'somewhere' is interdependent with the environmental, economic, political, social, familial and domestic conditions in which they live, and the personal resources available to them.

A primary element of salutogenesis is the 'sense of coherence'. Antonovsky defined the sense of coherence as increasing capability for managing, comprehending and making meaning of lifeworld circumstances. He reasoned that a strong sense of coherence would move individuals, families and communities towards the 'ease' end of the ease/dis-ease continuum during stressful times. This is precisely the point and the purpose of this book – navigating our way to managing, comprehending and making meaning of the lifeworld circumstances of ageing mothers of adults.

Salutogenesis aligns with Kathleen Galvin and Les Todres's dwelling-mobility theory. Like salutogenesis, dwelling-mobility delivers a clear nod to fluid definitions of health and wellbeing. Dwelling-mobility admits an existential component to Antonovsky's theory whilst sustaining fidelity to his idea that wellbeing is in constant flux. Dwelling-mobility describes wellbeing as a dynamic and ongoing exchange between 'rootedness' (dwelling) and 'flow' (mobility).

In 2020, researcher Julia Coffey published a theory of wellbeing designed to rattle complacency in research, policy and service delivery. She called it 'wellbeing as assembled'. Wellbeing-as-assembled, which I have hyphenated for clarity, contests strategies that advocate individual responsibility for health and wellbeing. Wellbeing-as-assembled is relational and embodied, with emphasis on the ways in which wellbeing is felt. Coffey recognises that felt qualities of wellbeing are critical to understanding health and wellbeing, and that felt qualities are rarely mentioned or explored in research inclined towards single-minded psychological and cognitive pursuit – which is almost all psychological and behavioural theories dominant through the past century and longer.

## Languaging

I like verbs. I like the connotation of do*ing*: movement, action, change evoked by the fusing of 'ing' to the tail end of static nouns. We can write, but writ*ing* will get us a book. We can paint, but paint-*ing* gets us a picture. We can sing, but it is sing*ing* that gives us a song. Language: the words we might speak. Languag*ing*: the speak-*ing* of the words available to us. The words available to us. Did you catch that? The words available to us. *The words we have available* *to us* when we are calm are unlikely to be the same words available to us when we are enraged or when we are sad. The words available to us when we know we are invited to speak freely are quite different to the words available to us when we tread on eggshells as we speak, if we speak at all at such times, in which case we may have no words or locked-in words. The words we had available to us when we were young and strong and empowered and unbeholden to clan, or beholden only to the point of self-interest, are not the same as the words we need now when the status of ageing mothers of adults is sidelined to 'useful, not included'.

When we write we can erase and rephrase the words we use. Delete, rewrite. Delete, word search, rewrite. We have no such luxury when we speak. When we speak, the words are out there. When we speak in touchy times, we may take a good deal of care with our words, thereby rendering our words tense with self-imposed limitations of silence and silenc*ing*, allowing for the possibility of more than one silence, and/or the do*ing* of silence with its inherent potential for undoing or not-doing silence. When we speak in touchy times it's possible that no matter what we speak we will be misconstrued, wilfully or otherwise, by the one or ones to whom we are speaking. This renders our speaking meaning-less or without meaning or usurped by malignant ill-meaning. When we speak in touchy times it is likely we will censor ourselves if we speak at all. If we are opting for the safe(est) route in touchy times, at the quartermark of the twenty-first century we rely on text sprinkled with pre-set emotional icons, *emojis*, to convey sentiments. Emojis are designed to speak for us. They are digitised human responses, stand-ins for the words we might speak if we were brave enough to put our voice in the world. They are also pre-set stand-in responses for the hurried and the too-busy, scant nothings masquerading as attention.

We are losing our words. Current generations are losing words they never had. Pre-determined digitised responses such as emojis, content sharing and AI generated responses to texts and messages are stand-ins for human engagement. When you are speaking to the whole world, you are speaking to no-one. Sharing content is not sharing when we withhold the words that tell others why the content we shared is important to us. We do this in part because we know we will get no languaged response to the sharing through which we sought human engagement. Sharing is not sharing when we do not know or have no interest in how the content was intended or received. Whilst the act of sharing is an attempt to connect with someone, the content itself is a stand-in for our own words and ideas. We are losing trust in ourselves for languaged public expression (words). We are hiding behind and relying upon the words and coded messages of icons and algorithms to speak for us.

Emojis are the dying breath of common courtesy. A heart or a thumbs up or a wow is not a meaningful response. For the ones who won't risk their words in digital space, emojis at best mask absent-mindedness, inattention, digital addiction and/or, at the other end of this silencing spectrum, bewilderment, uncertainty and shame in the glaring light of looming languaged exposure.

We live in touchy times. We are losing our language. If we ever had it at all. If we are children or among the ageing and elderly we are more likely to be spoken for and at and to, rather than mutually engaged in conversation, consultation or discussion. The meaning-less illusions of egalitarian engagement afforded children in our times don't count. For example, asking children if they want a bath then spending half an hour convincing them they do when they say 'no'.

Ageing and elderly versions of such perversions of languag-ing range from speaking childishly to ageing and elderly women to 'advising' them what to do based on your own interests – time avail-ability, unspent financial reserves, genuine disinterest. But this is not a book about how we speak to children or the ageing and elderly. It is a book about the nature of languaged longing and loneliness. It is a book about what it feels like to be without languaging for the bewildering state of 'ageing mother of adult children in a modern western industrialised family, and economy', and it is a book about what it *feels* like when our languaging – our words, our speaking – is unwelcome.

I loathe them.

We live in a world licenced to turn on the mother. A world in which that same mother has no right of reply. We all know the trope: *you know what mothers are like*. It is as if there is an offensive category of human labelled 'mother' and everyone knows what 'she' is 'like'. It is only in recent years that insight and adequate reply have come to me: *No, I don't. Tell me, what are mothers like?* Why did it take so long to frame such an obvious response? As any wounded mother of adults will tell you, it takes a great deal of courage to ask an honest question of these men and women we raised. They dismiss. They diminish. They shame. They sideline. Small, near meaningless barbs that accumulate over time in the bodies of ageing mothers of adults. Worse, they fling these tiny arrows in front of the children, the beloved grandchildren to whom we have given our hearts and in many cases our lives. Best we stay silent. Best we keep our mouths shut. Best we show up in the spaces allotted to us. You doubt my thesis? Ask an ageing mother of adult children if you dare, and give her room to find her words. If you dare.

Why dare? Harriet Rubin has your answer:

> "Young men in myth go out and kill the beast.
> Few ask: 'Who is the beast?'
> The answer: 'The ageing woman, back with redoubled strength'."

The ageing woman who finds her voice is a force. An entire generation of ageing mothers of adults who find their voices is a revolution. Politically. Socially. Economically. Familially. No longer willing to settle for useful, not included. First, however, she must find her words.

I loathe them.

What might Kate, an ageing mother of adults, mean when she speaks these words? Perhaps she means she is life-savingly desperate for genuine conversation with someone, anyone, about her experiences of being the mother of adult children in our society. Perhaps she means she is distressed to the point of longing-to-die rather than live another day with the pain of adult children and grandchildren who have turned on and away from her. Perhaps she means she is utterly bewildered about what is so awful about her that this is where fifty years and two generations of service has led her.

A refrain from the voices of many women included in this text is, *what did I do?* So I ask you. Does Kate loathe them? Or is she a woman without words in a society that does not allow the experiential speaking of ageing mothers of adult children? Does she loathe them? Or is hers the loathing of the walking wounded with no words other than those which turn on the ones who wound her. Does she loathe them? Or are her words a shorthand of sorts for the unworded agonies she has been living with these past years. Perhaps she says she loathes them by way of giving voice to the self-loathing she endures in consequence. Or perhaps her words, in the moment of their speaking to New York City Rose, were flippant words she thought were funny, given their uncommon usage in the context of ageing mothers of adult children. And now we know. Her words are not funny. *They are unacceptable.*

For Kate, before loathing in her feeling body, there was 'bewildered', the constant tear-full state of bewildered/bewildering. When we do not exist for those we love, we do not exist. Do you remember your grandmother's eyes? I do. My grandmother standing at her garden gate; her mother, my great-grandmother, withered with age beside her. Their eyes like pale blue stones I couldn't read. My mother too. Standing at her own gate. Hazel eyes, no withered mother beside her. They are gone now. All three of the women I knew who were older than me are now ashes and bone. It is I who stands at the edge of family time, no garden gate, no withered mother beside me. It is I who wears my grandmother's eyes, looking at the world through my body her body. Stone blue. Eyes with nothing left to say.

My grandmother's last words were these: *"What was that for?"* I used to think this was funny. A kind of enlightened spiritual wtf. Now my grandmother's eyes are my own, and they are my mother's, and my great-grandmother's. The eyes of the motherline, the family fractal. Mine to bear. Mine to live the astonishing pain of bewilderment lodged in retina, all that love, time and resourceful effort, the endless bountiful giving that came to this scorching, merciless fire of judgement unleashed from the adult children we birthed and to whom we gave our lives. That's what it was for. There is nothing any of us have done that is commensurate with their behaviour. We did not see this coming.

As Kate said. Bewildered.

Hand-in-hand with bewildered, she said, was 'loathsome'. *She* was loathsome. A shitshow of shame. There is and was and must be something so abominable about her that she was and is unworthy of time, respect, support, interest, care or thought from the ones to whom she has given her life. She had and has no idea what that abomination is or was, and she lived with that venomous force inside her body for many years. *What did I do?* They, the force of adults she birthed and raised, and their children, were obviously in some kind of collusive agreement with each other. After all, *she* is the one on the outside, therefore *she* must be the loathsome one. Therefore, according to the populist narratives of our time, *she* needs to take a good look at herself. And she did. I promise you. She tore herself up on the inside, cacophonies and choruses of shame and self-loathing pounding her internal shore. For years. And years. And years. All the while showing up with a smile and a brave face, picking her way around landmines and over tripwires, high tensile wary of saying the wrong word, making the crummy suggestion, offering the unacceptable wisdom.

The transition from loathsome (her) to loath*ing* (them) saved Kate's life. Loathing, unlike loathsome, was a short phase. She has no word yet for where she is now. Literally, no word, no words. For the first time in time that can be measured in decades she is peaceful in her body. She makes no effort to contact her adult children and grandchildren and the silence is no longer terrible. Or loathsome. Only occasionally is it bewildering. On her seventy-third birthday she turned off her phone so she wouldn't hear it not ring. They haunt her, to be sure, these wraiths that shadow her days and nights. Sometimes she measures days without a single sighting or haunting or thought or wonder, and she doesn't know if this is triumph or tragedy. She has no words to describe how she and her family got to here. No word. No words.

Audre Lorde says her silence will not protect her.

Hurt, shame, loathing, bewildered. These are words. Words in a body. They are not language. The communicate nothing. They are silent. They have not protected her. She has been fighting them for every breath. She has been fighting them for her life.

For the past ten years I have worked in the obscure and fuzzy field known as 'writing for wellbeing'. In that time I have sat in writing circles and online groups with thousands of people who do not identify as writers. In an attempt to understand the work and render the field less fuzzy I spent three years researching and writing a PhD. There were two questions I sought to answer: Why do people who do not identify as a writer drive hundreds of kilometres for a writing workshop? (Most of my work was in the Australian outback.) And why do people leave a two-hour writing workshop walking taller than when they walked in? The answer is in the dominant demographic drawn to my work: ageing women. Ageing women longing for languaged expression in the world *as they know themselves to be*. Ageing women aching for validity for who they know themselves to be. Ageing mothers, desolate in their being, craving their adult children to know them as they know themselves to be. Ageing women who know their complicity with the family story is killing them. Ageing mothers who hope to leave the grandchildren a different telling of who they are in the world. Ageing women with no words. And all the words. Ageing women seeking voice and visibility. Ageing women who know their silence has not protected them.

What ideas does the ageing mother of adult children absorb about herself when she is told she is supposed to 'get on with her life'? *They are her life.* What ideas does she absorb about herself when 'we know what mothers are like'? Whose language will the ageing mother of adult children speak when she is useful, not included? Whose ideas, words and tropes frame her world when she is silent, invisible, side-lined, undefended? Simone de Beauvoir asserts the ageing and elderly have two personality options available to them: sage (kind, quiet) or 'an old fool in their dotage' (sharp, brittle).

Our world is awash in the language of policy and opinion makers: experts, bureaucrats and ad-men. None of which is any longer speaking to us, the ageing mother. After decades of having her existence defined and languaged for her, and not noticing or not caring or being preoccupied with the lives of her children and grandchildren, and living up to and failing everyone's expectations, it is only when the chickens of silence and invisibility come home to roost that the ageing mother of adult children finds she has no words for her own existence – and no one else does either. The emotion-words and theories of the psychologists and the new age spiritualists don't fit. They never did. The promise-words of the ad men and policymakers don't fit. They never did. The diminishing words of the adult children don't fit. They hurt.

One ageing mother who came to a women's wellbeing writing retreat longed only to buy a 4WD and vanish into a desert. She had recently had surgery for a broken heart. She should have been dead. The retreat gave her the bolster she needed to drive away. She eventually settled on the fringe of a distant township, as far from her adult children as she could be and remain on the same continent. She set her own expectations. She built herself a house. She began to write. She still dies that proverbial death by a thousand cuts on phone calls and text messages from her adult children. She stays upright in the desert as their tiny arrows bring her down. She is writing for her grandchildren, so they know her as she knows herself to be. She is finding languaged voice and languaged visibility, as she knows herself to be, beyond the shame, loathing, judgement, cynicism and not-enoughness reflected back to her from her adult sons and daughters. She is finding her words, some borrowed, some made up, some claimed and re-claimed from time. They are her words. As she knows herself to be.

Words are not language. Language is a system of communication. The purpose of language is to communicate. Language requires an 'other'. Communication requires an other who is listening and speaking back. Writing words allows for the possibility future generations will know the woman who built herself a house in the desert, as she knows herself to be.

When Susan Johnson published a book called *Aphrodite's Breath: A Mother and Daughter's Greek Island Adventure*, media stories hacked it to headlines with varying versions of 'I took my mother to Greece for a year'. Language, please. The pronoun: the journey shared transformed by populist clickbait to an insulting, powerbroking 'I'. Subtext: 'Aren't I wonderful risking this potential shitshow (*we know what mothers are like*)'. Around the same time Jenette McCurdy published *I'm Glad My Mom Died*. We all know why the publishers sanctioned this title. Permissioned. Languaged. Licenced. McCurdy and her entire generation permissioned, languaged, licenced to turn on the mother, a trend that is accelerating with clickbait such as Harriet Shearsmith's article titled *'I cut my mother off so I can be a better parent'* and the recent release of McCurdy's book as a television series. You don't have to read McCurdy's book to know why she's glad her mother is dead or Shearsmith's article to know why she exiled her mother. Freud's end game. *We know what mothers are like.* People think adolescent girls are mean. It is not happenstance that the mother in these books is the mother of adult daughters, fair game and feedstuff for publishers' profits. Mother as monster. Mother as myth. Mother as clickbait, and we bit.

Daughters create their mothers just as surely as mothers create their daughters. McCurdy told Drew Barrymore she wanted a title people would find funny and would grab attention and would speak to people who suffered overbearing parents. There is no human woman who is mother in McCurdy's story. McCurdy's is the cardboard cutout mother of psychoanalytic myth. A woman whose 'faults' are mirrored in the sicknesses of the society that created both mother and daughter, as if one woman is responsible for the ills of her time. A daughter, by the way, who is benefitting from the same worth her mother imagined for her. Ironic, isn't it, that her greatest fame came from the mother she loathed who provided her with the skillset she now harnesses to fulfill that promise of fame.

All success stories are overcoming stories. The greater the success, the greater the overcoming. Paradoxically, in the Drew Barrymore interview, McCurdy was talking to a woman who achieved more stardom as a child than almost anyone since Shirley Temple, a woman who might also draw licence from our times and blame her mother for missteps, misjudgements and misdeeds, real, exaggerated and imagined. A woman who is still benefitting from all her mother imagined for her and who did not appear to find McCurdy's title as funny as McCurdy does. I look forward to McCurdy entering the realm of the ageing woman. Should she become the ageing mother of adult children I anticipate the apologies she'll be sending on the winds to a heaven she may or may not believe in.

Who will speak for the ageing mother of adult children if not the ageing mother of adult children? Facing mortality, the self-described black warrior poet Audre Lorde observed that what she most regretted in her life were her silences. In speaking of the pain of silence, and death as the final silence, Audre was speaking the heartwords of the thousands of ageing mothers of adults drawn to my writing workshops seeking voice in the world:

> "I have come to believe over and over again that what is most important to me must be spoken, made verbal and shared, even at the risk of having it bruised or misunderstood. We can sit in our corners mute forever while our sisters and our selves are wasted, while our children are distorted and destroyed ... we can sit in our safe corners mute as bottles, and we will still be no less afraid."

Silence, betrayal, death. Every ageing mother of adults who speaks, speaks for the first time. Simone de Beauvoir summoned us to shatter the "conspiracy of silence" about ageing. And yet, the language of psychology is the language of men, young men of wealth seeking to legitimise their ideas as 'science'. For more than a hundred years now psychology has built itself a house on ideas whose legitimacy was challenged at the time and are no longer challenged in corporate universities who churn out experts who have yet to leave home.

In the 1970s Australia threw open its university doors free of charge to anyone who wanted a degree. For a decade this funnelled the words and ideas of young and working class women into the mental health industry. It is only now that ageing mothers of adults are contributing in numbers to languaging the ideas that have framed and are still framing their lives, as the rising number of ageing women doing PhDs across the western world brings audibility to the words, ideas and voices of women long excluded from the naming and priority-making of power. To what purpose when those ideas are built on the same languaged theories that have brought modern western societies to the brink? It therefore may or may not be coincidence that along with the change and challenge that invariably accompanies ageing women into the system, the drop-out rate for ageing women is significantly greater than for their younger peers.

Unexamined populist tropes peddled by people who know nothing about the lives and experiences of ageing mothers of adult children silence the voices and shatter the spirits of the already silenced and shattered. Tiny arrows. There is no ready answer in defence of the apparent faults and failures of the ageing mother of adult children. When every woman who speaks speaks for the first time, women are always speaking as individuals about socio-political and familial avalanches that are systemic and buried with and within us in the destructive rubble of unexamined pop psychology. Dumb ideas built on dumb ideas built on dumb ideas until they enter the language and are repeatedly piled on those who are subdued by the still-young with agency.

When Greta's adult daughter told her to 'get on with her life' she was whiplash silent. *There is no other life.* She had been raising children since she was twenty-two years old. Her daughter had two children by the time she was nineteen. She was a grandmother at forty-two. She is an ageing mother who spent all her adult years giving to, caring for, listening to, running around after, cleaning house for, singing to sleep, shopping for, cooking for, sharing adventures with and loving children, adult children, grandchildren and adult grandchildren. There was no life that was not children and grandchildren. And beneath the avalanche of belittlement she hears the knowing sigh of the un-matured expert, 'ah yes, that would be empty nest syndrome':

> "(The construct) of "empty nest syndrome" was clinically identified and popularized in the 1970s as a group of symptoms including depression, loneliness, and low self-esteem, found among mothers whose last child had recently moved out of the family home." From, Encyclopedia of Aging and Public Health, 2008.

As if the 'problem' is hers, the empty nestee. As if the value she placed on caring and nurturing had value while it/she was useful, to be unmasked as the reality that she belongs inside the modern western family unit only on the basis of her usefulness. She never did belong as the enlivened woman she was, and is.

Whose language is this that makes foul fault of the dedicated mother? The baby bird has flown the nest. Boohoo the generations of mothers not allowed to work or study and then boohoo the ones expected to work and study and compete in a workplace that admits them entry on terms designed to exclude and break and profit from them and either she or they or nobody is thinking of the children. Boohoo the ageing mother of adult children in a western industrialised family, and economy, who in our linear world sees only the backs of her adult children and grandchildren marching off towards the horizon of 'their' life. They are doing precisely what we raised them to do. What my mother raised me to do. What my mother did. And as I look back down the motherline I am witness to the ever-decreasing responsibility to and for the ageing women of the motherline, until the final separation played out with my adult granddaughter severing herself altogether from the family line, a linear parade of diminishing returns. All this refusal to respect the ageing motherline, empty fucking nest syndrome, how's that working out for us?

So what does it mean to find language for, to give language to, to name? Finding language for is not the same thing as giving language to, and while either may or can be helpful there will be a price to be paid by the spoken-for for the latter. Neither finding language for nor giving language to are the same thing as naming. To name is to claim. To possess in one word: *mine*. We have witnessed the outcomes when 'mine' plays out in the husbands and fathers who claim naming rights to family lineages of women and children. And through the prodigious eighteenth-century sailors of Europe who floated over the horizon to plant their flags in 'the new world'. And the women and girls at the epicentre of medical and psychoanalytic theories, pronouncements, experiments and 'cures'. And the entire western industrialised world in the era of the rise and the rise of the mental health industry. Naming power. A disorder for everyone. An interior crisis for everyone. To name is to claim, to give meaning to, to know, to possess, to empower, to make visible, to own. It's the language of time, reverberating and subtle. Who tells the best story wins. Ageing mothers of adult children do not win. Winners have words.

When the spoken to and for are without language for their own living, effort is required to listen as they – in this case we, the ageing and elderly mothers of adults – reach for the words that speak for our existence. It can take us time to find our words, for the words are beyond the realm of anything we saw coming. The women who trod these roads before us bit their tongues and wired their jaws and wrapped thorns around their exposed hearts and I for one am now willing to cut and tear my own flesh so I might reach the spirit of the ageing mothers now gone and know them as they knew themselves to be.

Adult children do not give us time to find our words. The ageing mother walking on eggshells is unlikely to speak anything of what she intended or knows she must speak. When every woman who speaks speaks for the first time, we have nothing to build on. Contrary to what plays out on our screens, we do not live television lives. Our lives are unscripted. The adults we raised are not listening patiently while they wait for us to deliver our lines with aplomb, insight and 'truth' so well-expressed that tension dissolves and we are embraced for all time in recognition and love by the adults we raised. No. Ageing mothers are finding words in a breathless room crackling with the sparks of the fault-finders, waiting for their gavel to fall. Patience is required as we find new words for new ideas and ancient reckonings that transform unformed feelings of timeless hurt into words.

A vicious phrase has entered our English-speaking modern western world. It is a common phrase among adult daughters, and sons. 'My truth'. Or 'your truth', commonly expressed as 'well that's your truth'. We seem to be under the illusion that this small idiom is a settlement, a 'that's that', the end of the argument, the obvious and final word on the matter. We are at peace. Nothing to see here. 'My truth'/'your truth' is weaponised cowardice. It is dismissal. It is a failure of courage. It is unkind. It is without heart. For hidden in the shadows is another word: 'versus'. Versus = against. Inside every 'my truth' is a hard line separating 'my truth' from 'your truth'. Me, here and righteous. You, over there, wrong.

When 'truth' is wrapped in a story there is no truth, not one that can be fully described or understood. Given the short span of a human life, and the vast and myriad influences that are outside our line of sight and beyond our control, the reality is we will never know the whole of what's going on, from geographical and social conditions to political climates and generational family dynamics to an entire cosmic otherworld beyond our westernised ken. The reality is we are part of a matrix. There is no me without you. At best, when we pronounce 'my truth' we are saying *this is what I need to believe to keep my head above water*, a life buoy grasped in a stormy sea *because I don't know how to have this conversation*. At worst, 'my truth' is a declaration of family or community warfare, a hurtful attempt at high moral ground, a refusal to recognise our place in the scheme of things.

It's not uncommon in our times for the still young and the empowered middle aged (the adult children at the centre of this thesis) to claim words are 'whatever they mean to each person'. Um, no, no they're not. If our words are whatever they mean to each person, then we are at the mercy of mercurial assumptions and without means of communication. Words have meanings. In the words of philosopher Peter Kingsley, "(words) have power because they contain their meaning and significance inside them". The challenge is finding the words that align with our living. For example, is desire the same as longing? Sort of, perhaps, but no it's not the same. Is longing the same as wanting? Nope, it cannot be. Wanting is focused on what we do not have; longing is within, we already have it. Is longing the same as lust? Not the same. What of yearning, is longing the same as yearning? No, no it is not. Yearning is whimsy. Longing has a name.

Words have specific meanings. They are the yard stick by which we might measure the wheeling light of the sun. Without bearings the measurements become meaningless. Meaning always requires words.

This, this word, this is the word that speaks for me, and here, here are the many words that form the language that communicates the context of my living, and the context of my living includes you. There is no me without you. The nest is never empty.

It is time to rework the language of our living, for all our sakes in western industrialised families, and economies. And it is the ageing mothers of adult children to whom this responsibility must fall. For it is only ageing mothers of adults who have the dual vantage points of the silenced/disappeared *and* the empowered knowingness that comes with care of and love for and devotion to generations over time. It is only ageing mothers and grandmothers of adult children who are capacitated to recognise generational patterns languaged not by scientism and ad men but by life itself. Ageing mothers know what it is to be wounded over centuries and love anyway. I knew my great grandmother, my grandmother, my mother, my daughter, my granddaughter. That's a lot of living memory in one ageing woman's bones. Ageing mothers know what it is to turn on the ageing mother and then become the ageing mother. This tormenting strength is written on our retinas. It is our superpower.

## Longing

Longing is a wraith. Reviews of academic literature show that for all scientism's obsession with dissecting, categorising, defining and ordering emotions and feelings, it has neglected, overlooked or wilfully ignored longing. Rejected by the not-yet-passed age of reason as having no place in science, human longing went the way of emotion. Unlike emotion, longing has yet to make a comeback. Indeed, it appears science has paid more attention to wraiths than to longing. Non-theological literature on longing is scant. And then it's not. It's everywhere. We just don't call it longing. And yet. Look deeply enough into the pantheon of human emotion and you will find longing is the river beneath and bedevilling the entire repertoire of human emotion, behaving in all the ways a river might behave depending on the weather and the climate of its nights and days. It can feed and it can kill. It can nourish and it can overwhelm.

At the turn of the twenty-first century, astonished by the absence of longing in psychological literature, Swedish educator Olle Holm published an explorative paper attempting to position longing on the scientific emotional map. I say 'attempting' for no reason other than Holm's paper located and relocated longing around varying orders of emotions, so as to dissect and discuss its relational place in the established emotional scheme of things.

Holm's paper was published in English. I'd be curious to know what longing – *längtan* – is to the Swedes; not the dictionary definition, but rather the contextualisation of längtan inside their living. And I'm curious to know why or how Holm noticed or felt the absence of longing in the literature. Why did it matter to him, humanly rather than academically, and what delineations did he draw between longing and the myriad synonyms those less attuned to the nature of longing will intersperse in its place? I'm also curious about his motivations, given his paper focused on six-year-olds and adults barely have language for or comprehension of or awareness about longing, let alone adults picking at the minds of children. Mostly, I wonder why 'longing' is considered an emotion at all, which perhaps explains Holm's failure to pin this tail on that particular donkey. Framing these questions around Holm is incidental. The questions are the point.

What is longing?

For Holm and myriad other scholars, longing has an externalised object, specifically, as per the six-year-olds in Holm's study, longing for another person. For Holm, longing is passive. He has missed his target. Longing cannot be located outside the self. Longing is an interior force. Longing is the d/river on the inside. We do not long for something other than or beyond ourselves. That would be desire, yearning, wishing, wanting, seeking.

So if longing is not longing for an externalised 'other', what is it? My doctorate explored the relationship between wellbeing and writing. The research was underpinned by an eighteen-week writing program undertaken by sixteen adults, fifteen of whom were women who were middle aged, ageing or elderly. The exception was a trans man in his late twenties. Sixteen adults drawn to participate in a writing program group study. Why? It is too easy to say 'because they wanted to write'. We are a literate society. They can write. They can write perfectly well. They've been doing it since they were children. So why were they drawn to a writing program? At the time I began writing *Mothercry* I had been running writing workshops for ten years. In that time around three thousand literate people, almost all of whom were middle aged, ageing and elderly women, were drawn to these programs. Why? They say 'I can't write' when they demonstrably can write. To return to my research, for that is where the evidence lies, what drew sixteen literate adults to a writing program? The short answer is 'longing'. Again, it is too easy to say, 'longing to write', although there is that, too.

What were they longing for?

Longing has two branches: longing to (act) and longing for (the feeling that comes with acting – fulfillment, however momentary). The shape of longing belongs to the individual. The shape of longing has no shape. Longing is within. It is yours alone. No-one can describe it for you. You will never know what it truly wants from you. No-one can fulfill your longing for you. No-one can save you from your longing. It is yours to do and yours to feel and yours to not-know and yours to act on. Longing asks everything. It can be tasted but never realised; it cannot be put to bed.

So what were participants in my study longing for? Self-aligned expression in the world. Visibility, as they know themselves to be. Self on the page. Mirror mirror, a reflection I recognise. I exist. Longing requires we take action on our own behalf, and this they did by signing up for the writing program. They acted for their longing by seeking support to find the words they needed to language their living.

Longing requires us to show up and to keep showing up. Longing is an active force inside the human body that is commonly pre-language and, perhaps, without recognition. Activated longing demands we be brave. Actioned longing stirs up change. Acting on longing grows trust (in self) and fosters courage (to act in the world). Acting on longing transforms lives. Acting on her longing compelled our seventy-something woman with the broken heart to build a house in a northern desert (trust). It braced one study participant to tell her ex-husband he could no longer stay in her home when he was in town (brave). It propagated confidence in the heart of a trans man to observe "I can be attractive" (love). It emboldened the writer spirit of a farmer to honour the summons within and prioritise her writing over fruit picking (it's your inheritance, you manage it).

Western science is pathogenic. It is focussed on what's wrong. Longing is salutogenic by nature. It is solutions' focused. Actioned longing is heartening and strengthening. It builds capacity and capability in individuals, families and communities. Unactioned longing is withdrawal, from self, from others, from the world; the withheld self, contracted and cranky; unchecked, eventually to wither; until, the end game, longing turning on the body doing the longing (science word: depression) to eventually long only to die (science word: suicidal ideation). Unactioned longing enkindles suffering.

In fact, longing may be the artesian river feeding all scientific and academic study. As with wraiths, however, longing is beyond the purview of scientism. Longing's lament is the realm of the poets. Longing addressed through reasoning minds such as those of modern western industrialised scientists will never pin a flag on longing. Students of longing almost without exception interchange longing with desire, yearning, wishing, wanting. In this sense, Holm, like philosopher John McGraw, makes no distinction between actioned and unactioned longing. For McGraw, longing is the "intense wish" for removal of distance separating the self from what or whom is desired. Thus he confines longing to wishing. Holm trusses the human spirit to longing as passivity. The poets empower longing as pied piper to suffering. They are not entirely wrong. But longing is not lament. Lament is lament. Lament is longing indulged. Lament is longing's coddled song. Lament is longing unactioned. Lament is romanticised rumination. And to ruminate is to pick at sores.

The sixteen adults who signed up for the research program were longing to write. In the context of their longing, they knew instinctively that writing would deliver them visibility in the world. In stepping forward for their longing, they knew what would be asked from them: exposure. At last, their willingness to act on their longing was greater than their fear of exposure. At last, their longing for self-aligned visibility in the world won out over their desperate need to hide, to keep hiding, to remain hidden, silent. Why desperate? They knew the journey would expose long buried shames, fears, unworthiness. They were terrified of what lay ahead and yet they stepped forward. This is what longing asks from us. It is no small matter. They can write. They can write perfectly well. And yet, the terror. The terror lay not in wanting to write but in longing to write what matters. Self-aligned expression on the page. *Self.* On the page. The terror lay in the exposure, and they knew the writing program would expose them, to themselves, to their facilitator and to each other.

And it did. Over eighteen weeks the study's participants experienced prolonged agonies of serial exposure. And they wrote. They wrote through their shame. They wrote through their worthlessness. They wrote through their fears. They showed up. And they kept showing up, for themselves and for each other. Self as gift exchange.

In the entry interview to the study prior to the start of the writing program, I did not ask for personal or demographic information other than location. Instead, I asked one primary question: What drew you to this writing program group study? One question. Sixteen lives laid bare to a stranger. One woman was housebound with her husband's chronic PTSD. Her longing for reprieve took the form of writing a 'book of goodness' for her sons, to remind them there was more to life than the darkness that had descended on their home. Another was an ageing grandmother immobilised on her lounge by chronic addiction to digital media and gaming; her longing for inclusion took the form of writing a family history. The trans man living in a remote desert town writing poems of darkness and depression in his room – he longed to 'be' a writer. The unpartnered mother of five small children who lost everything they owned in a bushfire; she longed to share her heart with the world. An ageing farmer bound to a husband debilitated by stroke who longed for release from an old story etching itself into her skin. The hospital manager whose previous experiences with her internalised writing demons had left her twice her weight and near-divorced; she longed to share her management skills through writing the business manual that had taunted her for a decade. Others were middle aged women with children enduring divorce and reloca-tion who longed to write to make sense of their living. Another farmer, who had replanted and re-bridged her property following a flood only to see her reclaimed life wiped out in the next flood; she longed to write and write and write and write her body empty of distress. Sixteen adults seeking support for a proficiency each and every one of them possessed. Sixteen adults who knew what they were up against in acting for their longing.

Longing is a tension between ease and dis-ease. If acted upon, longing will move a person, family or community towards the ease end of the salutogenic continuum. Longing denied will glide us towards dis-ease. Actioned longing is an initiating force, a mobilisation of the internalised self towards being (well) in the world. Unactioned long-ing is destructive to human health and wellbeing. If not acted upon, longing has the potential to slay resilience and joy.

Longing is the dominion of the psyche, the Greek word for soul. Longing cannot be the work of either the scientists or the poets, for in its entirety it is beyond the ken of reason or lament. Longing, as we shall discover below, is work for the philosophers.

To act on longing is to take right action. It is to will change. It is to act transparently with no agenda. Actioned longing asks commitment. It requires surrender. To act for one's longing is to stand courageously in the fire of the next step and fear burning and burn yet not burn anyway. Acting on longing requires no justification, no excuse. Longing illuminates the narrowest of pathways, with each step revealed only when the next step has been taken. There is an end game, to be sure. It is longing's holy name in your psyche, and it is the light on the horizon calling you home. Between here and there, however, are countless distractions, pressures, claims, beholdenments, collapsings, collisions, betrayals until we understand, in the words of wizened Rose, the longing is the path. No-one can walk this path for us. No-one can save us from this path. The path of longing is yours and yours alone.

The self-aligned expression in the world humans seek is actioned longing. The transformation, wellbeing and 'authenticity' (pop guru word) humans hunger for is found in actioned longing. Longing is not wanting. Wanting, grasping, desiring, lusting, yearning, wishing are petty thieves come wearing balaclavas or, as is the case for most of us, dressed as wolves in sheep's clothing offering illusions of 'safety' (stay where you are, better the devil you know). Longing is the work of psyche. The longing is the path. Everything else is Snow White's poisoned apple come knocking at your door. In a world where every woman who speaks speaks for the first time, languaging the longing of the ageing mother of adult children is our first task. Languaging loneliness is the second. First, however, loneliness must be recognised for what it is – cry from the bitter hunter and hymn from the wounded heart.

## Loneliness

Loneliness is inseparable from longing. And like longing, loneliness is a latecomer to scientism's focus. Like longing, loneliness is notoriously challenging to define. And like longing, loneliness has been clinically observed to be relative to an object, an unfulfilled desired 'other'. Colin Killeen's 1998 paper marking loneliness as an under-researched epidemic appeared at the turning of scientism's tide. This was soon after Mother Teresa declared loneliness to be the most pervasive disease in western societies, defining it as "being unwanted, unloved and uncared for", and a decade before John Cacioppo and William Patrick identified loneliness as a high risk factor for early death, right up there with obesity and smoking. Loneliness did enjoy a wander in the academic sunshine during the 1950s with the work of, among others, psychiatrist Frieda Fromm Reichmann. Famously, Frieda was the tenacious doctor in the novel that was really a memoir, *I Never Promised You a Rose Garden*. Frieda observed that "loneliness seems to be such a painful, frightening experience that people will do practically everything to avoid it".

Unlike longing, loneliness is not subsumed by its synonyms – loneliness is just plain loneliness. And unlike longing, loneliness is trending for redress in public policy and discourse in mainstream western economies grasping for plausible budgetary solutions to the apparent mental health crisis. In 2018 the UK government published a report on loneliness which illuminated Cacioppo and Patrick's finding, that the impact of loneliness on human health was equivalent to that of smoking, which of course is another budgetary nightmare for the health portfolio. The implications of this finding were made manifold by the ensuing avalanche of papers associating loneliness with tension, stress, anxiety, neuroticism, shame, depression, self-loathing, dementia, immune system dysfunction, and so on. We are neurologically wired for social connectedness. Loneliness can change the mammalian brain.

The UK government's loneliness report mentions lonely/loneliness thirty times. Not once does it describe what living lonely *feels* like for the human body doing the living lonely. There are no synonyms for the word lonely. There are words that ascribe states-of-being to lonely, such as isolation, melancholy, alienated, abandoned. These words describe loneliness outcomes, and may or may not be relevant to the experiences of individuals. As a word-of-meaning lonely is just plain lonely. It says nothing about lonely to the not-lonely and it says terrible terrible inexpressible things to the lonely.

Psychologist Ami Rokach describes acute loneliness as a "terrorising pain, an agonising and frightening experience that leaves a person vulnerable, shaken and often wounded". Killeen defines loneliness as a "traumatic state of being" that is the "distressing, depressing, dehumanising, detached feelings that a person endures when there is a gaping emptiness in their life". Compare these statements with Letitia Anne Peplau and Daniel Perlman's 1982 definition of loneliness as the discrepancy between a) one's 'real' self and how others perceive them, and b) one's desired and actual relationships. For Peplau and Perlman, loneliness is an objective clinical condition with an obvious solution – close the gap. For Killeen and Rokach, loneliness is an experience that describes pain, hurt and anguish existent on their own terms inside the living human body. Interrogating loneliness from a distance has resulted in the development of scales and objective measures. These scales and measures, by their nature, avoid pain. They will not bring us close to what psychiatrist Ludwig Binswanger, a contemporary of Frieda Fromm Reichmann, described as the "naked horror" of loneliness.

Frieda stalked the currents of what she called 'real' loneliness in her clients. She distinguished real loneliness from culturally determined loneliness, self-imposed aloneness, compulsory solitude and isolation. She determined that real loneliness was discrete in that it was incommunicable. In other words, the other lonelinesses in her repertoire have words. They have a state of being in the world that is visible to others, and communicable words through which to address this state of being, even if the individual experiencing them is silent. Yet, as per the UK government report published sixty years later, all the lonelinesses are thrown into what Frieda described as "one terminological basket of 'loneliness'".

I am calling on Frieda's concern with real loneliness to excavate the buried agonies of ageing mothers of adults. This is not to suggest that ageing mothers of adults have a monopoly on real loneliness, nor to suggest that the other lonelinesses are irrelevant. The other lonelinesses are painful, too. And they are visible. And they are well-researched.

And those who endure them have amplified voice in the world, even if it is not their voice. And they are funded for redress, however inadequately. And they can result in "creative or scientific products" and as such may not be experienced as lonely during the period of constructive/creative isolation but become loneliness as a consequence. As such, constructive/creative isolation may be temporary, and even voluntarily entered into. The other lonelinesses have a seat at the Cabinet table, at least in the UK via the Ministry for Loneliness. The other lonelinesses have what Frieda astutely identified as a "common fate" and this common fate warrants their redress, at least collectively.

Real loneliness is "naked horror" loneliness. By Frieda's reckoning, it is private, it is incommunicable, it cannot be shared by empathy. It is terrifying. It is profound. It is tragic. The naked horror loneliness of the ageing mother of adults is not (necessarily) the naked horror of Frieda's professional extremities. Indeed, it may be considered an indulgence to position the ageing mother of adults in the realm of Frieda's real loneliness. Nonetheless, I am entering the ageing mother of adults into this ledger, however temporarily, for the ageing mother of adults is at this time enduring unvoiced exile. Her interiorised loneliness is severe. It is private. It is incommunicable. It cannot be shared by empathy. It is a rest-of-lifetime sentence. She did not enter into it voluntarily. It is terrifying. It is profound. It is tragic. There is no constructive reward. It is naked wtf horror and it will be removed from the ledger of real loneliness upon elevation to everyday loneliness with a seat and a voice at the Cabinet table.

In order to get a grip on real loneliness, thereby deepening our understanding of – and increasing our vocabulary for – all the lonelinesses, it is crucial to explore the nature and condition of real loneliness. Real loneliness is incommunicable for four primary reasons relevant to this thesis: 1. its private nature, 2. the conviction she is alone in her experience, 3. fear of recalling and thereby reliving her experiences, and 4. society's refusal/disallowance of what she would say if she could speak/had words for her experience. Real loneliness is a state of involuntary exile, a disappearing from view for the one who is real lonely. This disappearing is exacerbated by the likelihood that those around the ageing mother of adults are likely to be terrified of what she would speak if she could speak. Thereby, they "erect a psychological wall of ostracism and isolation" around themselves, and thus her exile is complete. Frieda contrasted this to the jester of the medieval court, who was licensed to speak unwelcome observations with candour, audacity, valance. Conversely, those in the orbit of, in this case, the distressed ageing mother of adult children, are prone to protecting themselves from her. *They do not want to hear what she cannot speak.*

Living is relational. There is no I without you, no me without the world. That rich seam of German philosophical thought and terminology in the late nineteenth and early twentieth century gave us 'the welts': the *umwelt*, the *mitwelt*, and the *eigenwelt*. The umwelt is the biological world we inhabit, our environment. The mitwelt is the world of our social relations. The eigenwelt is the private world of self, the world inside our skin. This is the matrix within which a person lives. Where does one welt end and the 'other', another, begin? Ultimately, there is only the welt. There is only the world. No I without you. No us without the welt/world. If living is relational, then meaning is always situated in the world. Who I know myself to be is only possible inside a relational matrix.

Real loneliness is the loss of the relational world. Binswanger observed this as the place where "love and friendship lose their power". Note the subtlety of Binswanger's distinction between object/other and interiorised meaning-making. It is not necessarily the loss of love and friendship that results in loneliness, it is the collapse of comprehensibility. Meaning has lost its way in the umwelt, and the mitwelt, to launch its final assault on the eigenwelt. Meaning is "despairingly exiled from the home and the eternalness of love and friendship". Meaning has "isolated itself" from "human traffic". Understanding is lost, for understanding is "only possible from continued interaction". Meaning withdrawn from the world 'traffics only with itself'. It becomes "a sheer Medusa-like stare", akin to what Rokach described as self-alienation, "a feeling of inner void, a detachment from oneself, and an alienation from one's core and identity". Hence we observe the potential for the catastrophic salutogenic slide towards dis-ease – obesity, smoking, mental terror – as the sense of coherence crumbles and life loses meaning, comprehensibility and manageability.

Like Frieda, Binswanger was concerned with extreme mental terror, known at the time as schizophrenia. As I said, it may be perceived – and is – an indulgence to claim the extremities of mental terror for the state of the ageing mother of adults who is uncomplicated by severe psychosis. Nonetheless, I persist. For what are the eyes of my grandmother and great grandmother if not set in the stone face of the one who traffics only with herself, "despairingly exiled from the home and the eternalness of love", where meaning has "isolated itself", the implication here being intention on the part of the exiled one, a self-aware withdrawal, a 'there is nothing for me here', an 'I can take this pain no more', an 'I will survive, I will stay living, I am visible in form though I traffic only with myself'. My grandmother lived for twenty years in this state, mute as Audre Lorde's bottles, alone in a house she cleaned every day. My mother was renowned for her kindness. At her funeral the farewell parade lined up to sprinkle 'kind' like confetti over her coffin. One word for a woman's lifetime. She was 'so kind'. Where my grandmother cleaned to ward off loneliness's threat to her sanity, my mother cultivated kindness as mask and battle shield, her lifeline to keep from falling into the dark well of loneliness from which the war within was sprung.

In seeking the words I would speak at my mother's funeral I came upon words she had written about herself. The first four words were these: I am a traveller. To others, my mother's entire life was condensed into the personification of 'kind'. Thus silenced, she trafficked only with herself. To herself, my mother was a traveller. The woman unseen. Disappeared by family and society's projection of who she was and ought to be as an elderly woman. Simone de Beauvoir made clear my mother had a choice at this stage of her life: sage or fool. Despairingly lonely, the traveller settled on kindness as currency for what little human engagement was left to her in the world. Thus my mother and grandmother warded off what Frieda determined to be the panic that parallels real loneliness, panic that is a constant and determined threat to sanity.

The UK Ministry for Loneliness released its fourth update in 2023. It hosts photographs of smiling faces of the two demographics at highest risk of loneliness, the young and the old. There in the report we find the ageing and elderly on buses and in gardens, accompanied by happy quotes, insights from committed caregivers and friendly ministerial visits. It is a document whose ministerial intentions are vote-catching and whose brief is threefold: reduce stigma, drive a lasting shift in social wellbeing and expand the evidence base. Its focus is measurements and scales. Its ontological foundations are unexamined. If you are feeling lonely, the report (should the lonely have read to the end) proposes you, 1. keep in touch with the people around you, 2. join a group, 3. do things you enjoy, 4. share your feelings – but don't compare yourself to others, and 5. help someone else feel connected ('be kind'). And if you feel you cannot action these steps, "be patient" and visit their website. So said the not-lonely. So said the empowered still-young and middle aged on career trajectories. So said the empowered still-young and middle aged in their best voice to elders about whom and about whose felt living state they know nothing.

Activities of no genuine interest or meaning will not 'solve' loneliness in a society constructed to create that same loneliness. Activities that drop the living lonely at their door, there to enter another night and day and night and day alone will not 'solve' loneliness. The ageing and elderly are not children who need activities to keep them busy, aka, salve for bureaucratic, political and familial consciences. Presuming the real lonely overcome their Medusa-like stare, the proffered activities are time-fillers. They may fill two or even ten hours of the one hundred and sixty-eight available to a human being in a week. They change nothing when the contextualised conditions of their living remain unchanged.

Besides, the ageing mother of adult children may not appear to be lonely. To the world she may appear to be engaged with and enlivened by her family. She has no need for 'activities'. To the outside world she is at the hub of family life. Several things can be true at once. For example, the ageing mother of adults can appear to be engaged with her family whilst feeling estranged from that same family – useful, not included. The ageing mother of adult children can be bathing grandchildren and cooking dinner with a smile on her face while her heart is breaking for her loss of place inside that same family. The ageing mother of adults enduring non-visible estrangement is held in muffled bondage by romanticised impositions from the world regarding the wonder of her lifeworld. She is an unlikely candidate for the UK ministry's measurements and scales, due in no small extent to what Simone de Beauvoir identified as "self-deception and pride … people don't want to say they are lonely".

Furthermore, Frieda Fromm Reichmann made it clear that "people who are in the grip of severe degrees of loneliness cannot talk about it", and those who had experienced such loneliness in the past were unlikely to do so either, "for it is so frightening and uncanny in character that they try to dissociate the memory of what it was like". Moreover, need it be said, the ageing mother of adults is protecting not only herself (from further shame, judgement), she is also protecting her adult children (from the miscalculated judgement of the world).

There can be no survey question that makes sense to the ageing mother of adults in a world which denies her experience, and therefore no scale upon which to place her experiences. Consequently, the experiences and voices of ageing mothers of adults are unlikely to be found in the brochure-like report on loneliness. In this one cavernous agony of loneliness, the ageing mother of adult children, non-visibly exiled from the family hearth, is alone in the welt. There is no-one to whom she can speak, for what can she say in a world unprepared for the actualities of her existence, a world unwilling to fathom her words, a world that refuses, rejects, disallows that which she would voice should she have words at all that amount to more than a complicit *yes, you're right, I am so very lucky,* and its breathless shadow, *what did I do?*

## The longing-loneliness nexus

Longing and loneliness are inherent to the nature of being human. They are the forever interior companions born with us into life. They are phenomena intimately tied to the work of existence. Psycho-analyst Melanie Klein proclaimed loneliness to be a "ubiquitous yearning for an unattainable perfect human state". Psychiatrist Frieda Fromm Reichmann described "ordinary" loneliness (that which is not real loneliness) as an existential fact. Nursing researcher Colin Killeen declared loneliness to be "part of being human and that will never change". Psychologist Ami Rokach determined loneliness to be "as natural and integral a part of being human as are joy, hunger and self-actualisation". Scholar Karin Dahlberg declared loneliness an "enigmatic phenomenon" that "belongs to life". Philosopher John McGraw, like Klein, viewed loneliness as a type of longing, referring to it as "the longing of loneliness". Much of the literature on loneliness will mention the word 'longing' without defining its context, meaning or purpose. Researcher Deborah Simonton states, although she did not necessarily intend it as a general statement, "while loneliness underpins (data), it is expressed as loss or longing".

Scientific literature assumes longing and loneliness to be emotions. The American Psychological Association defines emotions as:

> "… conscious mental reactions (such as anger or fear) subjectively experienced as strong feelings usually directed toward a specific object and typically accompanied by physiological and behavioral changes in the body."

It is inarguable that emotions exist in the interior of the living human body, and not just because the American Psychological

Association said so. The question is, is longing an emotion? Is loneliness an emotion? If longing gives rise to loneliness (McGraw), and loneliness is foundational to longing (Simonton), and longing and loneliness are ever-present in the human body, rising and retreating in intensity yet neither coming nor going as per all other emotions, then longing and loneliness may be reasoned to be other than emotion. Emotional triggers, perhaps, but not emotions.

If longing and loneliness are not emotions, what are they?

By skirting scientism's notice, longing has remained free to roam outside the boundaries of analytical dissection and dismemberment. We are at liberty to reject longing as a grammatically interchangeable emotion, and assert that longing is a vital force inside the human body unbeholden to externalised objects. So too loneliness, if we accept the observations of the analysts above. Longing and loneliness are therefore existent interior currents that are inescapable. They are within and they are inseparable.

Longing is an existent current that *gives rise to* its synonyms: desire, yearning, wishing, wanting, and so on. It does so either as diversionary straw men (save me from my longing) or paralysis (I'm not brave enough (yet) to act for my longing). Loneliness too is an existent force that gives rise to its not-synonyms: isolated, abandoned, alienated, and so on. To call these synonyms is lazy scholarship. Isolated, abandoned and alienated are not synonyms for lonely. They are conditions of living that are resultant from and/or causal to the living of loneliness. So too the numerous other synonyms proposed for lonely: deserted, destitute, empty, desolate, homeless. Longing applied obliviously has readily interchangeable synonyms, accessible everyday single words primed for mechanical insertion. Lonely has no ready synonyms, none that do not make cause (shame, blame, pity) through assumptions and judgement. Lonely is just plain lonely.

Longing and loneliness have languaging problems. Longing is the mudded jewel among the stones, unobserved and untreasured. *Mothercry* is a contribution to longing's rediscovery and recovery, its polishing and placing on the high mantle of human living. Conversely, loneliness is like starburst from a firecracker, its shoots and sparks need a taxonomy to better understand, describe and explain its nature, force and impact. As things stand, all the lonelinesses are 'lonely', whether they be Frieda's 'real' loneliness or the UK government report's 'needing companionship' lonely or the philosophers' observations that lonely is inherent to the humanness of being. All these lonelinesses, with no true words to distinguish one shade of lonely from another. Not in English.

Phenomenologically speaking, longing and loneliness are existent currents resident in the body of each and every human being as they navigate the welts. If this is so, then neither longing nor loneliness can be 'solved' or 'fixed'. Phenomenologically speaking, longing and loneliness are not their synonyms. The synonyms ascribed to them are emotional responses to longing and loneliness, in advance or retreat. Phenomenologically speaking, longing and loneliness are not states, for neither is static. They are streams, in flux and flow. They are energies. They are forces. They are dynamic catch-all terms that are vague, broad and inadequate by any measure.

Longing and loneliness are primal forces defined by their strength, power, ability and their capacity to perform something. It is this capacity to perform that determines longing's animation or stagnation, and lonely's not-synonyms (isolation, abandonment, alienation). This capacity to perform – or not – is the underbelly of the 'mental health crisis' draining the lifeforce from western industrialised families, communities, economies and health budgets, due in no small part to the synonymic confusion that has licenced twenty-first century mental health experts to neglect longing and loneliness's 'capacity to perform' (contribute to the world). Therefore, if longing and loneliness are principal currents resident in the living body, then it's possible longing and loneliness have potential to exact a far higher price than obesity or smoking as causal to premature death.

We live in unsettling times. Global unrest is on the rise. Philosopher

Hannah Arendt threaded the needle on the connection between lone-liness and the rise of tyranny and totalitarianism. Among the roots of political and social upheaval Hannah dug out loneliness, and, by asso-ciation, longing. In arguing that loneliness and isolation are a reflection of the relationship between self and world, Hannah stepped deep into loneliness territory and Frieda Fromm Reichmann's terror within.

One of the key findings in my own research is that diminished trust in self, others and the world withers the courage necessary to action longing, and will slide the individual (family or community) towards the dis-ease end of the salutogenic continuum. This slide results in withdrawal from the world, contributing to or causing social and fami-lial disconnection and estrangement. It also leads to or contributes to an individual's capacity to perform and the ensuant withholding of talents, gifts, endeavours, pursuits, interests and offerings. From here we can reason our way to isolation and loneliness as being analogous to unactioned longing, as expressed, for example, by the withdrawal of self from the world. From there we can reason that unactioned longing, left too long on the salutogenic slide towards dis-ease, is dry tinder to the totalitarian flame. *In extremis*, longing and loneliness unaddressed will lead to social discontent and eventually, if the lifeworld conditions are ripe, political strife. Whilst human longing and loneliness cannot be fixed or solved, Hannah warns us they can be lulled by good economic, political and social times. In times of trouble, however, unactioned longing and its resultant retreat from the world will fester to loneliness and its potential to erupt.

---

*Note: this text proposes Longing and Loneliness to be existent currents in the human body. From here on, they will be capitalised when referenc-ing the existent currents, in order to distinguish them from their small 'l' counterparts, longing and loneliness, and their synonyms/not synonyms.*

---

As an existent current in the human body, Longing is life's good-will ambassador. It is a lifeforce that calls upon us to heed the quiet, still voice within. Loneliness is life's existential intercessor. It is life's honest broker, mediating the line between hubris and humility. It can inspire imagination and map future possibilities. Loneliness is an existent current shadowing life's goodwill ambassador. Longing as an actioned force may summons us to pathways that lead out on a proverbial limb, at which point Loneliness makes ready company. Here, entwined on the limb, we find the growing capabilities of maturity.

The small 'l' lonelies, on the other hand, are emotional responses to lifeworld circumstances and events. Unchecked, they cause the honest broker to lose her way. Shame and unworthiness are nasty confidantes. Humiliation will upset the balance. So too hubris. The small 'l' lonelies have capacity to distort, distract, disrupt and attack, ruffians lying in ambush on Longing's trustworthy path. Longing and Loneliness immobilised, ignored and unactioned are toxic conspirators. Bored and drunk on their own power, they will make trouble within. Paradoxically, Longing as an actioned force can, with maturity and self regulation, mitigate the small 'l' lonelies, turning the enspirited body under attack to productive empowered pursuit.

There is a third force native to the human body, and that is love. Rokach addresses the small 'l' lonelies as yearning for love. This draws a direct line between the small 'l' lonelies and an externalised other. Psychologist Clark Moustakas identified the "terror and love" of loneliness. This love may be transmitted from a human being towards and into the living body of another, however perhaps it is neither the transmission nor the alleviation of loneliness that is the end game. Perhaps, the transmission is a transfusion, necessary to ignite the potency (strength, power, ability or capacity to perform) of love inert in the living body. Thus we find ourselves in existent current territory, what Dante described as "the Love that moves the Sun and the other stars".

Like longing, love is readily interchangeable with its synonyms: ardour, zeal, yearning, hunger, worship, infatuation, desire, appreciation, and so on. Like loneliness, love is 'one terminological basket of love', a catch-all word for everything from ice cream and pretty dresses to sexual attraction and approval. *Mothercry* contends that love, like Longing, is of a higher order than its synonyms. Love's synonyms, therefore, are emotional conditions that spring from love, lost or found. Love, as with Longing and Loneliness, has been miscategorised as an emotion. In fact, Love is a potency with capacity to perform something, in this case to realise Love's potential not as an emotion, but as a vast and powerful existent current within the living body.

The idea that Love, and by extension Longing and Loneliness, are existent primal forces beyond requirement for an externalised object has traction in Scandinavian scholarship. When Karin Dahlberg asserted that "loneliness is a phenomenon that belongs to life", she was affirming loneliness as an existent current. Katie Eriksson determined that human beings yearn to "be" love, and defined love as the energetic current between suffering and health. In so doing, she differentiated between Love as an existent potency in the living body and emotion-love as defined by its synonyms. Her theory mirrors the finding in my own thesis, that Longing is the tension between ease and dis-ease. Her construct also merges effortlessly with the salutogenic sense of coherence, thus emboldening the idea that Love, Longing and Loneliness are existent lifeforce currents with potential to slide a person along the salutogenic continuum towards ease or dis-ease.

The nexus between Longing and Loneliness is a construct without language. The nexus needs a word. Perhaps the Germans with their gift for life-words can help, or perhaps that word is Love. The nexus between Longing and Loneliness is Love. Triple potencies in flux and flow in the living human body, with the power to hurt or heal that same body. In synonymic form, longing, loneliness and love are: 1. selective regarding the targeted object or 'other' deigned worthy or unworthy of desire or attention (i.e., petty, exclusive); 2. tokens to be given and taken away (from a person, people or the welts); 3. undisciplined brigands laying ready ambush and tearing up the house; the crossroads between perpetual entitlement and maturity; 4. emotional revolutionaries setting fire to the world. Therefore, the qualities of Longing, Loneliness and Love as existent lifeforce currents endure without externalised reference. They are not only non-selective but without conscious capacity for selecting or 'choosing'. They can be consciously mobilised and directed within the living host body and extended beyond the host body into the matrix of relational living. They are toxic in stagnation, in flux without flow (contraction/withdrawal). They are empowering, restorative and satisfying in flux-and-flow (dwelling-mobility). They are never benign.

Salutogenically speaking, the existent currents of Longing, Loneliness and Love are inherent to the nature of living human. They are motivational forward propulsions to be either resisted, ignored and struggled with, or initiated and actioned. The synonymic aspects of longing (desire, wanting, yearning) forge a nexus with the small 'l' lonelies. Loneliness as an existent current is the tension that moderates longing's excess (hubris). The non-longing aspects of loneliness (desire, yearning, wanting, etc.), when unmanaged in the human interior, are the emotional revolution that burns down the house (the current mental health crisis). For ageing mothers of adults, mobilising and putting to right action the potencies of Longing, Loneliness and Love is the revolution within, a revolution that drags with it, into the interior of our being, a characteristically sticky challenge: to act for ourselves whilst sustaining consideration for others in our welts.

Phenomenologically speaking, the existent currents of Longing, Loneliness and Love are foundational to the mental health crisis troubling the worried well in modern western industrialised societies. They are cause and antidote for almost all the troubles, by any name: anxiety, depression, suicidal ideation, and so on. Analysts who ignore the potent, immutable currents existent in the living human body are failing themselves and their clients. Actioned Longing will lead us to Kingsley's 'other worlds', aka the unknown. And where Longing leads, the agentic currents of Loneliness and Love will follow.

The empowered ageing woman is a human being with her lifeforce currents in play. She is firing on the inside. She is Harriet Rubin's ageing woman back with redoubled strength.

## Writing

For most human beings writing is the bravest thing they will ever do. Writing what matters demands we enter into an ongoing process of overcoming. This ongoing process involves an edgy tango with shame and trust, courage and vulnerability, struggle and surrender. Entering into the process of overcoming invites enormous personal risk. This risk is punctuated by exposure of the withheld self, the archnemesis of which is judgement and the elemental forms of which are shame and unworthiness. To the withheld self, this possibility, this entering into, this preparing for, this overcoming, is excruciating. Through writing what matters an individual knows they will face the withheld self. It is a breathless place. What should be inside will soon be outside, on the page, loose in the world, evident to self and potentially to others. Writing makes witness to baneful aspects of self that the world has found wanting, and from which we ourselves turn and have turned. Writing lays bare our Longing, our Loneliness, our Love and all their small 'l' equivalencies.

Writing peers into shadows. Verb or noun, writing is neither innocent nor benign. In stepping forward to act for their longing to write, brave writers activate their willingness to overcome, to risk exposure of aspects of themselves they have hitherto rejected as unacceptable. They will be visible, witnessed, exposed. No longer hiding. One brave writer in my study described her experience of overcoming through writing as "like finding a huge pocket of pus somewhere that you didn't know you were carrying and letting it all go". This is writing as surrender, not to the writing program or any component thereof, but to the summons within the living interior of a human body.

In overcoming deep-rooted obstacles to expressions of self in writing, particularly in a group, brave writers prise themselves open to new ways of being in the world. They risk feeling not just their break-ing heart, but witnessing and feeling the breaking hearts of others. Breaking hearts are synonymous with qualities of vulnerability solidi-fied to 'stay safe', 'be acceptable' and 'avoid shaming'. Brave writers in my programs have swum rivers of shame as they weather the unbear-ability of the breaking heart, their own and others', from there to experience trust as the bridge from fear to courage. This is the transi-tional space where 'I'm not good enough', 'I'm useless' and 'I'm stupid' are transformed by the same tool that triggers or is deeply associated with these dreaded inadequacies: writing. Brave writers, defined as people who long to write who may or may not identify as 'a writer', experience constant tension between longing to relinquish control of interior voices of sabotage that hold them hostage and surrender to public exposure that which has previously been withheld to 'stay safe'. They risk and they weather the unbearability of the breaking human heart. And they do so not once, but over and over and over again.

These encounters with self, others and the world in a writing group are an interdependent process of gift exchange. It is an interchange of trust and self empowerment in writing. It is salutogenic gain and as such is foundational to brave writers' experiences of flourishing in the world. It requires courage to stand in the light of exposure and stare down malodorous fears and shames. It requires trust they will not be judged by witnesses to their discomposure and embarrassment. It requires conviction that the potential they quietly know is theirs for the claiming will be vindicated. Thus brave writers, through writing and ongoing public exposure, experience and transform their capacity for living in self-aligned languaged visibility in the world.

Writing is a process of self encounter. Mirror mirror on the (writing) wall. This is the mirror of ancient lore, tormenter and truth-teller, har-binger of whispered danger. Languaging the self in writing risks creating a material counter-self. Engagement with the material counter-self on the page risks slipping through the mirror into that which is unknown, is yet to be known or has been long-known but shunned or avoided.

Such slippages risk change: foreseen, foreseeable, unforeseen, mis-seen. Writing is a spillway, the point at which the see-saws of struggle and surrender, control and trust tumble from rigid worlds that keep the writer 'safe' into the watery world of human engagement. Brave writers discover "what's happening in my writing process is mirrored with what's happening in my life".

The brave writer who was focussed on writing a business manual for professionals found the short in-session writing exercises and home-work challenges catapulted her into reframing significant life expe-riences, including her abandonment at an orphanage as a child: "I just couldn't believe that such an enormous thing was coming out of one little writing exercise. I was really blown away by the power of it … somehow (this writing is) making other things easier."

Here we find the whispered danger of the mirrored self on the page. The ancient mirror precipitating upheaval then finding for our-selves, through languaging the self in writing, a safe place to land on the page. There is a place beyond safe landing on the page, where the written self arises from the page and takes a seat at life's table. It is the grandmother with her digital media addictions trading lethargy for meaningful purpose. It is the trans man turning his attention from poems of darkness to poems of love. It is the downcast teacher who writes her way to self-belief enough to trust she can resign and get another job. It is the unpartnered mother who lost everything she owned in the Christmas bushfires no longer "stuck" at the "boundary" of her own shell-shocked existence. It is the still-young woman with terminal cancer turning to the garden while she is sick, having used journal writing to realise: "I have to talk a lot kinder to myself."

There is relief and exhale in the recovery of self when voice and visi-bility are connected and claimed. It is writing as unsilencing, writing as retrieval, writing as renewal. It is writing as overcoming self-sabotaging behaviours through willingness to surrender to Longing. It is writing to endure challenges with the unknown and writing that contests habitual ways of being. Inherent in such challenges are encounters with risk, specifically and ongoingly the risk of 'feeling unsafe' and its counter-force, the calibration of interiorised self-reliance. Consequently through writing individuals develop increasing capacity and capability for trust in themselves as they propel themselves through writing into challenges with the unknown. It is writing as salutogenic process. It is salutogenesis as actioned Longing. It is actioned Longing as overcoming. It is overcoming as amalgamation of willingness and surrender(ing). It is surrendering through jagged though sustained movement towards the ease end of the salutogenic continuum.

At bedrock it is individuals experiencing for themselves through writing that 'feeling' unsafe is not the same as 'being' unsafe. They feel unsafe, they overcome. They trust. They progress towards their goal of self-aligned visibility in the world. They are safe-unsafe. They are writing. This three-step outline is entangled, not linear. The actualities of writing experiences are concurrent, simultaneously vulnerable *and* exposing, demanding *and* brave. The writer's willingness to show up for herself advances her Longing for self-aligned visibility in the world. Metaphorically, the writer's journey can be reified as wrestling with bears, overcoming that which has been unbearable and learning to live with collective (I am not alone) vulnerability and hurt.

It is simplistic to attribute the lifeworld outcomes for brave writers to writing alone. Writing is the medium. It is the pathway out and the pathway home. However optimisation of writing as a health and wellbeing resource is an assemblage (wellbeing-as-assembled) comprising five tangible elements: writing, guidance and support, access (the study program was free), the group and nature (the program includes writing in the world). The assemblage also includes one non-tangible element that is pivotal to health and wellbeing outcomes – the willingness of individuals to act for their Longing.

Writing is an affordable, accessible mechanism for human beings to intimately understand, manage and regulate the existent currents of Longing, Loneliness and Love as experienced in, by and through the living body. It is a health and wellbeing *practice*, aka, something to be practiced. It is a way of tracing risings and leavings in the body; a means for monitoring and managing Longing, Loneliness and Love before they become forces out of kilter. It is a method for putting these primal lifeforces to work on behalf of the human being in the world.

Phenomenologically speaking, writing is the only expressive tool available to human beings that languages in material form the essences of their interior living. Wayfinding the human interior through writing is an alchemical process. It makes real the unreal, it settles old scores, it releases toxins and tensions from blood and bone. It validates, it disproves, it legitimises, it rejects, it builds, it demolishes, it solidifies, it thaws. Writing makes a private record (however temporary) of the withheld self, reshaped, reformed, reframed, renewed, realigned as she knows herself to be. For the ageing mother of adults, writing is the long-held exhale. Writing in a facilitated group makes sheltered possibility for her visibility and her voice, as she recognises herself among women who are speaking for the first time.

## Languaging the feeling body through writing

Transformation is not exclusively a psychological process. Transformation takes place in the human body. Author Briohny Doyle observes: "There is no way to narrativise your way out of trouble; if anything, the more you narrate the deeper the hole." Story-making, what Briohny calls 'narrativising', is not the reason writing is good for human wellbeing. Story-making, narrativising, is a mental undertaking. Story-making might make us feel as if we've had our say. It might serve our agenda. It might deliver the righteousness of 'my truth'. It might offer a sense of strategising our way through challenges into new ways of being in the world. The reality is story-making is mythmaking. It is marketing for an individual's personal brand. The story we tell is always the story we can live with. Wellbeing-through-writing is not story-making.

Wellbeing-through-writing is a languaging process that leads us deep into the feeling spaces of the human body. Languaging the feeling body through writing is a way of finding words that align with our living, and these words are never a story. Stories have pronouns: she and he and they; she said, he did, they didn't. The feeling body's words are advocates for blood and bone and fat and flesh. They are unlikely to come in sentences. Stories have their place in the human scheme of things. As a method of embodied empowerment that's not it.

Briohny went further: "Narratives which prescribe empowerment … solidify things that aren't solid and reify things that aren't tangible." Languaging the feeling body through writing makes tangible not the story, but that which gave rise to the story, the origin-place of self-protective and/or self-defensive ways of being in the world. Languaging the feeling body finds communicable words for the origin-place. It finds words that match the self-aligned and self-defined essences of human living, demystifying and illuminating the drivers and impulsions of the interior of the human body doing the living in the world.

Bodies are how we know the world. Bodies sense other bodies. Bodies fail to sense other bodies. Bodies bump into other bodies, intentionally or otherwise. Bodies scar, visibly and non-visibly. Bodies hurt, through physical encounters, emotional encounters, psychological encounters and psychic encounters. Bodies hold on, to other bodies, to emotions, to trauma, to fear, to ideas, to beliefs – *bodies hold on*. Bodies let go. Bodies don't let go. Bodies matter. And yet, without the living spirit of the one we call 'person', the body does none of these things, but die. Psychiatrist Bessel van der Kolk describes the need for language to describe feelings in the living body:

> "As long as we register emotions primarily in our heads (*aka story-making*), we can remain pretty much in control, but feeling as if our chest is caving in or we've been punched in the gut is unbearable. We'll do anything to make these awful visceral sensations go away, whether it is clinging desperately to another human being, rendering ourselves insensible with drugs or alcohol, or

taking a knife to the skin to replace overwhelming emotions with definable sensations … the solution requires finding ways to help people alter the inner sensory landscape of their bodies."

Wellbeing-through-writing is writing what matters. The term refers in equal measure to journaling and writing the business manual a brave writer may have been longing to write for a decade. It is a method for altering the sensory landscape of interiorised living in the human body. Writing is the master key. Wellbeing-through-writing languages this sensory landscape, giving pause, privacy, recognition, validation, courage to stay with the gut punch, the caving chest; to be with the feeling body; to give words to, to bear the unbearability of and see the unbearability through. Languaging the feeling body in writing gives us words to demystify reactionary bewilderment. With words we can make sense of, we can manage, we can stay with and move through, delivering the living body respite and relief from overwhelming physiological responses to living.

To language is to know. To language is to name. To language is to make self visible to self, and, perhaps, to others who are willing to find new ways of listening. Wellbeing-through-writing is any writing that empties the human body of a story lodged in blood, bone, fat and flesh. It is writing that languages the feeling body. More than this, it is writing that languages Longing, Loneliness and Love as primal and potent feeling forces running sure as blood in the living body.

Know the potency, know thyself.

Languaging the feeling body through writing is defined as the use of writing to explore, identify and give language to pre-story feeling/s in the body. Feelings are not emotions. Distinguishing between emotions and feelings can be challenging. Feelings are what we feel in the living body. Emotions tend to be science words that name, categorise, measure, scale and know their place in the taxonomical scheme of things. Through this system, the naming of emotions has been given to us. The word 'anger', for example, is 'one of six primary emotions', or one of 'five', or one of 'twenty-seven', depending on your authority *de rigueur*.

These taxonomies stake pegs in the grounds of academic careers and are useful, perhaps, for theoretical explorations. They say nothing about the feeling body that is experiencing anger. Anger may have been hijacked as a word in a hierarchy of emotions, however what are the feeling words for anger? What are the body's words, *this* body's words, for anger? This is not to say there's no such thing as anger. It is to suggest that with exploration, a person experiencing 'anger' may find, with the time for exploration and experimentation that writing provides, that there are other words and feelings that may more accurately convey their experiences of feeling/s of anger.

Giving self-aligned words to feelings can be more than challenging – it can be strange, threatening, even terrifying. The trans man in the research program said the invitation to visit the welt inside his skin would "make me feel things I don't want to feel". This statement was not set in stone. Rather, it was a stepping stone. By the end of the program he stated he was going about his business in the world feeling "attractive" and "free". Attractive and free may tell us little about the experience of the body feeling attractive and free. They are, however, indicative of outcomes for a human being eventually willing to visit, and make peace with, the world inside his skin.

In the research interviews undertaken prior to the start of the wellbeing-through-writing program, I asked participants how they *felt* about writing, not-writing, about-to-be-writing. Fourteen participants did not understand the question. One paused, reflected, then said: "That's an interesting question", paused, reflected again, observed: "I've never thought about that before." When I asked another participant what it *felt* like not doing what she most longed to do, which was write, the conversation went like this:

Participant: (long pause). Ah, it feels bland. Disappointing and very heavy

Researcher: And what impact do you think that might have on your life?

Participant: It would definitely, keep me trapped and silenced

Researcher: And what does that feel like?

Participant: (big sigh). It feels um griefy, um feels like a loss and big grief

Researcher: Can you describe where in your body that you can feel that?

Participant: Ah, just in the solar plexus

Researcher: And how would you describe the feeling?

Participant: (deep exhale). Um. Tight. And distressed. And um, regressive

Researcher: So let's now imagine that you are doing what you most long to do and you're accessing that voice that longs to speak. Feel into that for minute, and

Participant: It's definitely in my throat

Researcher: It's in your throat? And what's your experience of that?

Participant: I just felt this beautiful clear, this clearway happen. It's like a, like an expansion of my throat. And I feel light and ah full of, full of song almost. Full of, like it makes me wanna cry with just how proud and fulfilled I am."

The feeling body's words are clear-eyed. They are strong and certain and calm, regardless of the emotional state they are describing. Again, they are unlikely to come in sentences. Languaging the feeling body invites us to speak beyond metaphor, avoiding mental constructs. It is premised on the idea that all emotional trouble passes through or lodges in the body. It is not speaking the mind's idea of the body, it is the body speaking for itself. Feelings are physical. They're not mental. They're not psychological. Feelings are what we *feel*. After that we tell a story and now we're in the realm of the mental, the psychological.

To make meaning of our feeling/s we tell a story, and more than likely this story is a set-up to avoid feeling and outsource its cause to the world.

Shame is a Longing inhibitor. Shame expedites and feeds the small 'l' lonelies. Embedded in the alchemical journey of wellbeing-through-writing practice is the idea that 'shame' and 'home' are resident in the same central place in the human body. Propelled by Longing and fuelled by courage, shame is the point of emergence into visibility in the world. It is an initiatory force that takes place in writers' bodies. It is a rupturing of the withdrawn self. It demands trust in the unknown and this demands courage. Always it asks for more.

Wellbeing-through-writing practice is a weaving, a dance of sharing and dwelling with. It is the building of community through recognising self in others. It is salutogenic insistence on speaking to strength and recognition of capacity in the name of being well. Giving language through writing to feelings experienced by the body will put human beings on energised pathways to solutions-focused living, regardless of and with heed for historic or current lifeworld circumstances.

All genuine personal inquiry is feeling body inquiry. It asks us to listen to our own body before we ask questions of other people about their bodies. It asks medical professionals to enter their own skin and listen to their body before pronouncing on other bodies. It asks health systems and the professionals who work in them to allow time for those in their care to find language for the feeling body. I have begun to imagine what everyday communications in families, communities, workplaces, bureaucracies and health systems might look like, sound like, *feel* like if people had widespread capacity for languaging the feeling body. More than 'fine'. Beyond 'I'm okay'. No longer constrained by 'good' or 'I have a sore throat'. I am left wondering if perhaps languaging the feeling body through writing might be the bravest thing we have left to do in our times.

Languaging the feeling body through writing is a phenomenological process. Scholar Julia Coffey stated that "sensory, affective and bodily registers are critical for understanding what wellbeing is". If this is so, then languaging those registers is critical to understanding and managing health and wellbeing. Languaging the feeling body through writing is the tracing through the dark. It is the point of readiness to begin the journey home, towards that which is longed for. It is more than thinking, more than ruminating, more than wondering and more than feeling. It is forward moving languaging that ferries the writer beyond 'what if' and 'I should' and 'they did' and 'they shouldn't' to the realm of actioned Longing.

## The omphalos of the ageing mother of adults

In the potent depth of the ancient temple of Delphi bode a sacred stone, the omphalos, the navel of the world, a point of vitalising power. In common telling Delphi belongs to the god Apollo. Before Apollo, Gaia. Delphi was and is a woman's place of power, wisdom, guidance. The omphalos is the navel, the bellybutton of the human body, the point of literal attachment to the human mother. Rabbi Susan Schnur described the navel as an "outward expression of self and lineage" that ought be revered as "placental mammals' most sacred site".

These days I am haunted by the joys of my mother's mothering years when her children were young. My mother birthed four children in four years in four different towns. She had married a man with an unpredictable propensity for violence, slim pickings for a capable, intelligent, adventurous woman nearing thirty who yearned for children at a time when marriage was her portal to babies and thirty was near-past acceptable childbearing age. There is no doubt those early years were difficult years. And yet, my mother loved her babies. She taught us all the things we needed to know: to throw a straight ball, to run with the wind, to read, to laugh uproariously, to read music, to swim, to drive, to ride horses, to play the piano, to navigate the world. She knitted us pretty jumpers. She made us moomoos we could turn inside out when we needed a clean dress. She never told us not to get our clothes dirty. She gave every one of us a birthday party every year, lining us up to make party hats and streamers, while she planned games for the classroom-full of children we'd invited. She said yes to life and taught us to do so too. We laughed our heads off. We yelled at each other. We gave each other a whack when words failed us and no-one was listening anyway. They were robust years with a mother who never stopped trying and always showed up. She did all this and worked full-time. And mostly what she got from the adult children she raised was criticism.

And then the dreadful silence when the hearth-noise died and, like my grandmother and great-grandmother, there was only my mother in her house. I can still see the urgency she flashed at me in her eyes about twenty years later when I visited her in an awful rental. It was a flash that said I am very close to finding a way to end my life. It was the flash that lights the point in every day when the tide of human affairs recedes, when streets empty, stores close and people retreat, as light itself withdraws from the world. It is the point where unpartnered once-mothers sit alone in houses and sip a glass of whisky as they blink into the shadows. It is the dimming of the day and the mothers of disinterested adults must adapt to silence. This shifting of the day, the tide of evening that transits light to dark, is a menace that casts forgotten ageing mothers adrift from all of life. They are left on the tideline, like sodden autumn leaves blown by the wind and unwanted plastic cups stuck in the sand, waiting for the tide to turn, to swallow them up again, to reclaim them, to note their existence in the burgeoning busy world of morning. I have felt that flash, although it was not a flash and of course I now know it was not a flash for my mother either. Or my grandmother. Or my great-grandmother. It was an unbearable state of being that we bore and bear anyway.

The omphalos of the ageing mothers of adults in industrialised western families is the junction where a full house of babies and children turns with swift and sudden shattering silence not to emptiness, but to *non existence*. This non existence seems to occur not at the point when the children leave, for they come and go for a time. It occurs when they are established in their lives, when they have homes and careers and partners and the self-important confidence of adults in their thirties, forties and fifties. It occurs when simultaneously we step forward for, or they nominate our availability for, grandchildren and childcare. Useful, not included. I will not bore you with the lost-to-the-world capacities of the women in my own family as age came to their bodies. Suffice to say, lest they be construed as cardboard cut-outs of mother, grandmother and great-grandmother, that these women weathered war and economic depression, one established Sydney's first maternity hospital and never lost a mother, another established maths centres, reading clinics and English as a second language in Australian schools, another ran a large home for girls in crisis, cooking thirty meals every night, another pioneered writing programs in isolated communities and gave voice and visibility to women's lives through newspaper journalism. Among many, many, many other things. *What more did we want from them?*

Their missing-from-the-world inspiration, capacity and commitment is not the point, although it is also the point. The point is that in industrialised western societies the adults we raise do not learn, as we did not learn, that they and we have an obligation to the omphalos of the motherline. This obligation is an ongoing cycle of return and renewal, in life and beyond the grave. It is living pilgrimage. It is worshipful, it is reverent, it is a polishing of the sacred. It is a listening for what she knows and sees coming that for all your empowerment in the world you do not yet know and have not yet seen barrelling down the line towards you. The living reality of the mothers is contained in the S words: source, sustenance, spirit, strength, sacrifice, surrender, silence. We had a right to every expectation that the children we raised would not turn on or from us. We do not know any of this until it is too late. We will live for all our days with this pain reaching up and down the motherline, up the line for the women I and we neglected and/or criticised and down the line for the bitter weathering of those to whom I and we gave our best life.

For Kate, the power of her adult son and daughters to hurt her eventually made it impossible to breathe. One night in the heart of darkness she woke to the weight of her own choked silence paralysing her chest. She could not breathe. She was content to die. She did not die. Grief's pressures had not brought on a heart attack, but a panic attack. After nearly fifty years and two generations of service, unable to bear the pain in her body any longer, she acted for her own survival. She did the unthinkable: she stopped initiating contact with her adult children and her grandchildren. For so very long she had feared that if she did not make the effort to phone or visit she would disappear from their world. The day came when she could hold on no longer. *This dreadful holding on.* A sort of wide-eyed broken courage warmed her blood. What would happen if she let go her fearful grip? Her greatest fear is they would not notice. She spent time that can be measured in years on that thought. *What will happen if I let go my fearful grip?* I'll tell you what happened. She was whistled away on the wind, like an astronaut cut loose in space. She was right. If she did not make the effort, she ceased to exist, unless and until they wanted her to mind the children, most of whom were by this time grown to adulthood.

Kate told me she recently glanced into the rear vision mirror of her car and stopped short at her face. There in the mirror was the down-turned mouth common to the ageing and elderly. Resting sad face. She stared. The corners of her lips were close to her chin. Her eyes were without spark. The world inside her skin was a vibration of deep sadness that filled the whole of her being. The whole of her. Resting sad place. The price of peace in the body of an ageing mother of adult children no longer holding on to people who have no interest in her.

Jo describes the disinterest of her adult children as like being a "cardboard cut-out". She says, "it's as if after they've visited they think I stay put exactly where they left me, as if I have no life in between their visits". There is the not very interesting fact of what Jo said, that she feels like a cardboard cut-out. Between the lines and spaces, however, are the actualities of what she is telling us. She describes the feeling in her body as like "a sucker punch". Her hand flies to her belly. Now are we getting her meaning? Sucker punches are illegal in Australia. A well-aimed sucker punch can kill. Sucker punches hurt. They really really hurt. And those that don't kill can seriously maim.

Kate and Jo are describing the actualities for the living bodies of two ageing mothers with five adult children between them, all five of whom are capable, courteous, high-income earning, well-liked people in the world. Resting sad face. Sucker punched. What impact the choked throat, the tight chest, the debilitating sadness, the ongoing sucker punches on the health of an ageing woman's body? Kate and Jo's experiences with the adults they raised is redoubled by the dawning recognition that what is experienced by their bodies, was also experienced by their mothers' unlanguaged bodies. Their silence has not protected them. Cross-disciplinary scholar Barbara Mor wrote of the long history of women's disappeared ways of being in the world: "We are tough and ancient, tried by a million years of ice and fire. On minute wheels of pain and beauty we have turned." Those minute wheels are the omphalos of ageing mothers of adult children.

Bodies, lest we forget, transmit. The existent currents in play in the human body are not confined to the individual body. They spin out as the currents of other bodies spin in. For the ageing mother of disinterested adults, resting sad face might be considered a brittling of the primal forces within as she makes ready for the sucker punches she knows are coming her way – or, enlivened by her joy at seeing or speaking with the adults she raised, she fails to remember the sucker punch is coming at all. Jo's body is a hive of punch-ready tension when her daughter calls, as Jo makes her body ready for not-saying 'the wrong word' or, god forbid, she talks about herself.

Laura's adult daughter had a second baby. Laura had already visited her daughter and newborn granddaughter. Nonetheless, she was passing by the hospital the following morning and decided to call in. The withering look on her daughter's face sent joyful Laura to bed for the rest of the day. Tiny arrows that bring a woman down.

We teach our daughters how to treat their mothers. At a moment of pivotal family urgency a while back I attempted to speak to my adult daughter about what I saw coming down the motherline. She snapped: "You think you're so wise." Tiny arrows. The family sucker punch came soon after. Resting sad face. Tiny arrows. They bring us down. We choke on our silence. Still we rise. The miracle of the ageing mother of adult children: *still we rise*. Still we stand, for you. Like my mother, and like my adult daughter, herself the mother of an adult daughter, we show up anyway, ever-ready for our adult children and grandchildren's return to the omphalos of the motherline.

Ageing mothers of adults know they must be their own witness. Hence their showing up in writing circles that offer guidance and support for channelling voice and visibility to the page. Mute as bottles, ageing mothers of adults know instinctively that writing will language that which has them by the throat. It is my prayer for the ageing mothers of adults, and my intention in writing this book, that we write a sky high library of words that languages our living for the unlanguaged ageing mothers of adults throughout the western industrialised world, and for our daughters, the ageing mothers of adults to come. This library will be the omphalos stone of our shattered times.

# 2.

## Contemporary Monsters

I T IS THE time of the pandemic and I am wandering along the river with Laura. Recent encounters with our adult daughters have us both bruised and bewildered. We trade tiny arrows. We are confounded by our daughters' 'mother', who is not an embodied woman of intelligence and good heart that either of us recognises, but a woman without significance, personality or worldview. I tell Laura I have a theory.

"They want the authority that is rightfully ours," I say.

"They want us dead."

We laughed, uproariously of course. Laura says I should put quote marks around 'adults'. That makes us laugh harder. Ageing women are famous for their cackling laughter. Crones as witch; weathered, withered, wild. You will never know until you get here what we find so funny.

Our daughters came of empowered middle age at a time of infinite possibilities for western women and for individuals. They are everything and more Laura and I not only might have imagined for ourselves, but gave over in our own lives so they might imagine this future for themselves. *I am not my mother*, thank you Nancy Friday. Our daughters are precisely who we raised them to be. Yet at this time we are no longer proud of them. Attitude-wise they are who we were at their age. We are shattered by our reflections in the fruit of our efforts.

To siphon off the words of psychologist and playwright Florence

Scott-Maxwell, mothers of adults are "under a painful law that the life that passed through her must be brought to fruition". By which words Florence means, at least through this lens, that we the mothers of empowered adults are right to expect so much more from them than *this*, and that this expecting is never done. It is biologically written into us. It cannot be otherwise until we are passed from this Earth and the expecting is theirs to do and endure. One might make an argument for Florence's 'expecting' as essential to the evolution of the species, were it not counterforced by the rise of an indomitable trio of contemporary monsters endemic to modern western industrialised societies: individualism, the privatised nuclear family and the mental health industry. These behemoths, reified by television and social media, have been gifted to the world by western and particularly American industrialists, entrepreneurs and tech barons unbeholden to community and motivated by profit. They have infiltrated, shaped, dominated, permeated and changed the lifeworld conditions of all the living creatures on Earth.

The aspirational standard of living in western industrialised nations was set throughout the twentieth century by Earth's dominant economic and military superpower, the United States of America. From the end of World War II, human ways of being in the world – who we are, how we behave, what we have a 'right' to expect – have been measured against the possibilities laid out by that simultaneously wondrous, arrogant, diverse, troubled, overcrowded, supremacist and hyper-individualistic populace that collectively we call, as they call themselves, the Americans. We aspire to be them as they aspire to be themselves. We and they mock their self-aggrandisement. We and they loathe their imperial ways. We and they want what they have and what they have is the constitutionally enshrined right to *everything*, on their own terms. Mine, by right.

The global cultural dominance of the Americans was accelerated by a technological miracle called 'television'. Since the 1950s we have lived television lives. Television compelled children off the streets and adults off shady verandahs to flickering screens and inside lives. It silenced conversation and set impossibly high benchmarks for living. Scriptwriters (predominately white American males), producers (predominately white American males), directors (predominately white American males) and actors (predominately white American males and white male-defined white females) beguiled us with lives not our own. They condensed time, scripted perfect retorts to people (actors) who appeared to be genuinely listening, manipulated emotional expectations and responses, choreographed bedroom intimacy and sculpted families and relationships. White American males decided who was on the screen and who was not on the screen, who was in a life and who was not in a life, what was said in a life to whom and about whom and what was not said in a life. They showed us what to wear, what to say, how to look, how to live, what to think, how to have sex, who to be and what we might expect. Television laid the groundwork for everything western industrialised people (future parents), and therefore generations-to-come, think they know about the world, as generations come of age and into adulthood through the profit-motivated lenses of the ad men and agents of promise, fantasy and illusion.

Television over time popularly defined what we currently 'know' about teenagers. Addendum: teenagers in the modern industrialised west. Television adjudicated and normalised the insolence and indolence of teenagers, as well as adult indulgence for the insolence and indolence of teenagers. In no other culture, generation or time in human history could a fifteen-year-old who refused to help around the house, get out of bed, pick up their own socks, speak courteously to those around them and contribute financially or otherwise to the household have presumed a warm bed and a decent meal at the end of the day. There is no other point in human history whereby an entire social stratum of young adults can behave this way whilst expecting – and receiving – three meals a day, education, money, a social life, phones, computers and fashionable clothing (washed and folded). In the 2020s, it is not uncommon for this over-exulted and over-empowered segment of western society to achieve this whilst rarely leaving their room. This is one television story that has slithered its way into mass consciousness and taught young adults how to behave and parents how to respond. The other story is of dispossessed teenaged men, lionised as lone wolfs or gang leaders.

Television legitimised and romanticised these broken possibilities for young adults, whilst adjudicating parental response and responsibility, commonly outsourced in our time to therapy or the police. What is the impact on – and the price paid by – a society that privileges, licenses, glorifies young adults whilst defaulting to their age and changes in hormonal status as excuses for demoralising and destructive behaviour that is caustic for themselves, their families and their communities? Are 'teenagers' and their families hostage to hormones as a 'natural' stage of life, or might the rise of the 'teenager' be an unmet hormonally-ignited need for self-reliance and responsibility expressed as frustration with the infantilisation of young men and women who ought to be making their way in the world, thereby developing accountability to, and capacity for living in self-alignment with, that same world.

'Adolescent' is the antecedent of 'teenager.' Both words, both concepts, were invented by the Americans. Psychologist G. Stanley Hall is credited with coining the term 'adolescence' in 1898, whilst 'teenager' is a marketing word invented in 1944 by Chicago businessman Eugene Gilbert. 'Teenager' was intended to exploit the spending power of young adults in the economic boon that followed the Second World War. Gilbert wanted to sell them shoes. Television exalted and emancipated what music historian Jon Savage describes as the "romantic idea of youth as a separate, stormy, rebellious stage of life". For the Americans, wrote Savage, the twin pillars of business and individual freedom are fundamental to the national identity. Savage observed that the mass-production of 'teenager' in the American psyche concocted an entire section of society unbeholden to others, "with its own peer-generated rituals, rights and demands".

Television's offspring is the internet. Television's grand-offspring is social media. Social media created possibilities for the entire world to script, produce, direct and perform their own lives. Not just adults, but children and babies too. Every breath a performance, a showcase, a chimera. For the first time in human history, technologies such as Zoom have given humans the capacity to watch themselves watching and engaging with other people watching and engaging with themselves watching and engaging with others. Are we getting a sense the snake is eating its own tail?

By the early 2020s, the American Centres for Disease Control and Prevention (CDC) reported 15% of American teenagers endured serious depression, whilst 22% of American teenagers considered suicide, 10% followed through and almost 3% succeeded. In a nation of 300+million people, the numbers of young adults in that brief overview can be counted in millions – to which can be added the millions more prescribed drugs for mental, emotional and behavioural 'issues'. Across the USA, currently 25% of adults have been clinically diagnosed with, and been prescribed pharmaceutical drugs for, 'mental health disorders'. In Australia, currently 22% of adults, around five million of us, have been clinically diagnosed with a 'mental health disorder', with 18% prescribed pharmaceutical drugs, most commonly anti-depressants.

Essayist and poet Robert Bly's concept of the 'sibling society' offers a sound analytic lens for viewing the current state of western social, familial and individual affairs. The concept speaks to the unanimity of culture that has resulted from American global dominance, whereby people across the world "listen to the same music, speak the same language, wear the same clothes, look at each other with envy and ignore grownups and little ones". The sibling society denotes a shift in human engagement from the vertical to the horizontal. The vertical society looks up: to parents, elders, leaders, ancestors, god; and down, to the monsters and demons found in cautionary tales and elsewhere. Whichever way you look, as with the omphalos stone of

Delphi, there is accountability, reckoning and guidance up and down the line. The sibling society is a horizontal society. It looks sideways, sees only itself reflected in the world. It is likely, says Bly, that 'siblings' in America feel closer to people they do not know in other countries than they do to family members in the same room. Bly credits playwright Michael Ventura with the following insight: "When Elvis wriggled his pelvis on the Tommy and Jimmy Dorsey show in 1956 all the parents in America lost their children on a single night." This singular idea is representative of a culture in which generations of adults have progressively abandoned themselves, their children, their parents and communities to "impulse gratification", the idea that one can do whatever one feels like doing whenever one feels like it.

Says Bly, "that seemed like a great victory at the time".

## Individualism

Around the time I turned fifty-five I remember thinking I ought to write a letter of apology to everyone to whom I had ever offered advice, in the spirited hope they had not taken it. The unweathered western young and middle aged, blind to ever-radiating cycles of life in play, oblivious to ripples in ponds from pebbles cast before they were born, are impervious to unimagined webs of relationships, unbeholden to unknowable human lives about to be impacted by guidance offered blithely by the unaccountable to the self-serving. The sibling society offers itself fulsome justification through aphorisms such as 'my right to' and 'your right to', 'it's my/your life', 'my authentic life', 'my truth', 'you do you', and so on. The sibling society is unbound by duty, care, obligation or responsibility to others in the vertical chain. The sibling society is beholden to self first and turns to its peers for guidance, typically underwritten by 'it's your life, of course you must ...'. Two everyday anecdotes tell us all we need to know about the sibling society, and the disparity between vertical and horizontal ways of being in the world:

In the 1980s, Jo packed up her small children and left their home in England for the distant southern shores of Tasmania. Realistically, she could not have moved any further from her homeland. She was twenty-three years old. She fled no great trouble, no war or famine. It was a bright idea she enacted cheered on by her friends without thought for the matrix of relationships she left behind and would be denied her children: her mother, their grandmother; her grandmother, their great grandmother; her brother, their uncle; the cousins and the cousins to come. Now the ageing mother of adults, Jo's own grandchildren are a world away and Jo is on the shoreline, reconciling the loss reverberating in her body with the decision she made fifty years ago.

In 2016 I was working in a remote township on the fringe of an Australian desert, running writing workshops with newly literate Indigenous adults. One young man, nineteen years old, was recently released from prison. The small story he wrote was one of worry: 'Who is getting food for my mum and my grandmother while I'm in jail?'

The cultural distinctions between Jo and the young Indigenous man are not incidental to their ways of being the world: the former horizontal, the latter vertical. Their ways of being are textbook distinctions between what psychotherapist Alfred Adler defined as 'private logic' versus 'community feeling'. Adler's use of the word 'versus', with consideration for translation, cannot be incidental when a simple 'and' might have sufficed. This is especially so among generations raised with popularised platitudes such as 'you can be anything you want to be' and 'you can have it all'. A friend's daughter, married and on maternity leave, with a baby and a five-year-old at school, and a husband who returns every evening, said exasperatedly, "how am I supposed to take care of two children by myself!" An acquaintance's daughter is a wealthy woman with two young children who each have their own nanny. Adler's 'versus' is apparent across a multitude of ripples in this particular pair of ponds, which echo Bly's lament: "We may be the first species to forget how to raise its young."

The privileged 'I' that is private logic is a modern western development in the pantheon of human history. Private logic is incidental to community feeling. Private logic is compatible with community feeling only so long as community feeling reflects or is in service to private logic. In the contemporary west, determining who 'I' am and how 'I' feel begins inside the skin of the individualised 'me'. For most of the rest of the world, cultural context still determines who 'I' am and how 'I' feel. Indeed, for most the world 'I' is an unknowable phenomenon without reference to group, family, clan. Cultural priorities, whether deliberate or embedded, are imprinted in language and rooted in community feeling. Community feeling is anathema to the lionised private logic of the western world.

Adler's contemporary, psychoanalyst Sigmund Freud, has been predominant in shaping a century of individualised thought and western ways of being. Freud privileged the psychic development of the individual on its own terms, whereas Adler rooted the psychic development of the individual in the world. Adlerian scholar Colin Brett states that for Adler, "social interest can be summed up in the phrase 'me with you' as opposed to 'me against you'". The latter, he added, would be the Adlerian definition of neurosis. Freudian supremacy amplified the illusion that private logic, me against you, is 'real', and licenced western academics, scientists, therapists and, eventually, everyday people to create and reinforce fictions about themselves and others, thereby unleashing swathes of concocted 'my truths' to shape, reinforce and peddle beliefs and entitlements in twenty-first century western ways of being to justify ruination of personal, family and clan relationships.

Private logic is an individual's internalised belief system. Therapy is always centrally focused on the individualised I/me. Adler observed that beliefs become the source of our inabilities. By this reasoning, private logic will restrict people from acting in the world. Adler also observed that 'private understanding and private language are also characteristics of the insane'; that obsession with private interests diminishes capacity for distinguishing between right and wrong; that this incapacity will result in lack of community feeling; and that private logic can justify anything.

Private logic is the warp and weft of capital 'I' Individualism, a philosophical movement mobilised in Europe in the 1700s. Individualism was a social theory that arose during 'the Enlightenment', a period characterised by a fresh attitude of inquiry and discovery. Individualism asserted the rights and interests of the individual as discrete from the tyranny of medieval institutions such as church and feudalism. Individualism championed the right of 'man' to think and act for himself (pronoun intended). Over centuries, the doctrine of self-interest has experienced a multitude of incarnations, ranging from an individualism rooted in society, to individualism as vital to competition and economic development (capitalism), to individualism as the over-indulged contemporary consumption-driven western 'I'. The tech giant Apple Inc. astutely stamped the nature of our times with its branding of a series of entertainment and utility devices: iPhone, iPod, iPad.

With the arrival of smart phones private logic was transformed into private universes. Ingenious algorithms pilfered and regurgitated data, fuelled generative outrage, compelled us to self-promotional lives, created illusions of genuine connection, spoke for us through quick-click word shortcuts and locked us into self-reflective content sibling-bubbles. The introduction of the iPhone in 2007 created limitless conditions of influential possibility for the social media platforms that dominate, superintend, indoctrinate, monitor, fuel, isolate, mediate and reflect contemporary individual welts.

We – adults and children across the age spectrum – spend inordinate amounts of time constructing identities, living inside fictional environments and performing our lives for others who are in turn performing their lives for us. In the west, 'community' is no longer "a world we are born into that is geographically coherent, sustained by shared rituals, implicated in every aspect of our lives and to which we have an obligation", as described by broadcaster and philosopher Waleed Ali. Rather, communities are purposively constructed around identity. They are lobby groups for special interests and self-interest. Private logic kingdoms. Me against you.

Ali's podcast co-host, philosopher Scott Stephens, references the Roman concept *munus* as "this thing that exists in between people that means that people who are born into the world incur a kind of debt, an obligation to other people as persons". Stephens distinguishes between traditional meanings of community and current usage in the west, stating that what was "deeper, richer and involved obligation has morphed into something that is individualistic and claim-making". Adults reorientating their lives, and their children's lives, around identity is a sibling move. Individualism is selective. Individualism reflecting itself to itself via narrowly defined 'special' interest communities creates insiders and outsiders, those who belong and those who do not belong, those who 'understand' and 'agree' and those who perceivedly do not understand or agree.

Individualism does not create community, it destroys community. In current social climatic conditions, siblings have capacity to 'block' anyone at all for any reason at all. We know why this action is necessary in the lawless realm of private logic unleashed in the digitised public sphere. It makes sense. Equally it makes no sense when children 'block' friends with whom they've had a disagreement in the playground and young adults 'block' parents and grandparents as an act of un-belonging: *I'm right, you're wrong, matter closed.* To block is to kill a person socially. When it takes root outside a social media bubble it is to kill a person's place in their community and/or family. Children and young adults who 'block' can unleash forces of collusion beyond their ken and control. Thus we experience the rise of the individual empowered to live without leaving their room. Everything can be brought to the door in a digital life, including meals, making 'friends' and severing relationships, without guidance, context or care for the impact of their actions on the world in which they actually live.

The sibling society picks and chooses to whom it is beholden and under what circumstances. We are, in the words of philosopher Ernest Becker, "tranquilising ourselves with the trivial" and creating digitised "monuments to our specialness". Actual community, that which is recipient of Adler's community feeling, is all of the people. Identity, regardless of purpose and however noble, is claim-making, and claim-making is dry tinder to individualism's looming climax as a (non)sustainable way of being in the world.

Philosopher Mark Fisher observed that western society has developed a memory condition, *anterograde amnesia*. This is the subversion of central narratives to the right of individuals to create competing stories framed in their own image. This has trapped us in content bubbles that make it impossible to orient ourselves to the world we actually live in. Culturally determinant movies, books, music, art are, through the 2010s and well into the 2020s, repackaged versions of big hits from times past. From Taylor Swift's Eras tour to the Marvel Cinematic Universe, we are living and reliving the age of nostalgia, trapped in a story loop. This includes Facebook memories and digitised accounts of our lives that ensure we never forget or evolve our memories.

In the meantime middle aged and ageing women come to writing programs seeking support to find their words, to write their way to making visible some sort of self-aligned expression in the world. They are hungry for a new accounting of themselves, for life outside the story loop, for recognition beyond other people's mean and narrow perceptions of who they are in the world. This is more than women wanting an artifact of private logic. It is a crisis of having no language for lifeworld experiences and the urgency of finding that language. Their purpose in seeking support to write is to transcend their experiences, not dwell amongst them or revel endlessly in the enduring agony.

Almost all women in the writing groups will, at some point in the program, murmur a version of 'everyone is great but not me'. *Everyone is great but not me.* Individualism's noxious symptoms made explicit in writing circles. Ageing women who seek to memorialise who they know themselves to be, exhausted by hogtied counter-selves measured against, compared to, competing with the over-exerted performance-selves of 'friends' in their social media feeds. These are overt displays of Adler's private logic desperate for community feeling. Says philosopher Slavoj Žižek, you can only love your neighbour if you can smell your neighbour.

The self-worship of the sibling society is individualism's end game, the fruit of the poisoned tree. It has to be. Siblings are refusing to grow up. With each new generation throughout the post-Second World War century in the west, a new wave of individualistic behaviour and moral attitude was born. We know them as: The war generation. The post-war generation. Boomers I. Boomers II. Gen X. Millennials. Gen Z. Seven popularly defined cultures in one hundred years, and counting. Sibling culture has left swathes of children with ever-diminishing parents, as mothers and fathers have in steady forward momentum refused to grow up and grow-with the increasing responsibilities of middle age, from there to grow 'old'. After all, 'you're only as old as you feel' and 'age is just a number'.

Further, the escalation of the favoured 'I' during the age of Boomer II created the monster of 'the inner self', another American invention that wormed its way into western human psyches in the 1960s and has since gobbled its way through every aspect of human life in the name of 'a better me'. Young adults cradle 'my' depression and 'my' anxiety like a baby or new dress, as if these states of being are obvious and tangible and surely and rightfully belonging to them in this embodied life. And now, the end game – individuals turning on themselves. The children are taking knives to their arms. They are depressed. They are anxious. They are drugged. They want to die. The mothers and fathers are turning on themselves. They are depressed. They are anxious. They are drugged. They take their own lives. The ageing and elderly look back in horror at what they, we, all of us in the west have inherited and propagated that is largely without name or language for the collective confusion and despair we know we are witness to yet internalise through the perpetual self-obsessive 'I'.

The potential for individualism's harm in the west and westernising societies is reflected in an ancient Egyptian tale, *The Sorcerer's Apprentice*: A sorcerer takes on an apprentice, a young man learning the craft. One day the sorcerer leaves the workshop to do business elsewhere in the neighbourhood, leaving the apprentice in charge of the workroom. With limited experience and no guidance, the apprentice begins tinkering with forces he doesn't understand and cannot control. He unleashes maniacal trouble in the world and the sorcerer returns just in time to save the day. The sibling society, filled with self-reflective hubris and broken by the maniacal trouble it has unleashed in the world, cannot save itself. The sibling society, blind to its horizontal ways and ignorant of the savagery of its contrived individualised language, is destroying itself by the same efforts it makes to save itself.

If we are to agree that individualism is a significant problem in the industrialised west, then treating individuals for systemic challenges can only, by definition, destroy individuals who seek relief, respite, salvation *from individualism*. Bly may offer us a way out. He leans into the first recorded version of the folk tale *Jack and the Beanstalk* to illustrate the importance of the vertical to human society. In this earliest written version, Jack (fatherless son) trades the cow for beans (sibling behaviour) and receives a dose of "good female mother anger" (parenting). The mother throws the beans out the window, they grow (the vertical) and Jack is summoned up the beanstalk by a crone (Harriet Rubin's ageing woman back with redoubled strength). The crone knows Jack's family backstory (ancestral heritage). She tells him the family's treasure was stolen by a giant (television/social media) and where he can find it (beyond the individualised 'I'). Jack risks confrontation with the giant (rite of passage) and retrieves the treasure (maturity).

Bly points out most cultures protect their children from the giant. Western societies feed their children to the giant.

## Nuclear family disaster

Individualism's fertile soil is another industrialised western contribution to and imposition upon humanity: the modern nuclear family. Just as current usage of 'community' represents a fracturing of actual community, so too the modern nuclear family denotes a fracturing of 'family'. Philosophers, historians and academics may argue the toss about the nature, history and value of the modern nuclear family, nonetheless there are three reasonable assertions that can be made: 1. the modern nuclear family is romanticised and reified as the epitome of love, support and place of belonging; 2. the modern nuclear family is an economic unit that is foundational to corporate capitalism and therefore vital to the generation of the material resources of individuals in an industrialised society; 3. the modern nuclear family is an aberration in human history – for most of human time we have lived in kinship groups, clans, tribes; in much if not most of the world, we still do.

The modern nuclear family dissociated from a matrix of nuclear families is the breeding ground for individualism. It is a privatised unit of individuals comprising mother, father, child/ren, led by siblings whose self-determined sense of agency and resultant emotional immaturity corrals the children from meaningful and reciprocal relationships with kin, including and particularly, given their largely non-visible status in the west, their elders and ancestors. In the modern nuclear family grandmothers are not family. They are 'extended family'. In the non-westernised elsewhere, including inside westernised nations among the usually not-white, grandmothers are family. A Palestinian woman interviewed on a podcast spoke of thirty-two members of her family killed by the Israel Defence Forces during its years'-long and counting obliteration of the people of Gaza. Thirty-two people has tremendous shock absorbing capacity for personal troubles in a family, and by 'shock absorbing' I am not referring to the ongoing tragedy unleashed on the people of Palestine. Thirty-two people in a family is anathema to children raised in western industrialised families, where grandmothers, aunts, uncles and cousins are not family but 'extended' family. The western industrialised family is a privatised unit whose children are raised in financial, social and emotional bondage to their parents.

Sally knows what I mean:

> *"I was on a hike up a steep hill with my son, his wife and their two sons. As we were catching our breath at the top, the youngest child, who was six, stood up and pointed to each of us one by one. He started with his mother at one end of the line. As he pointed, he said: 'I love you' and 'I love you' and 'I love you' and 'I don't love you'. I was shattered. The 'don't' was for me. I have an incredible bond with this child. I've had him with me since he was a baby, regularly and often, sometimes for months at a time. He has been taught he is supposed to love his family and 'family' is the small number of people he counts as mother, father, brother."*

The modern nuclear family is expressive of a language of possessiveness and a culture of power. It mistakes ownership for love. In these particular ways the modern nuclear family is unlikely to differ from all family structures. In the modern nuclear family, however, the language of possessiveness and the culture of power is rooted in individuals, not the group. Sally wasn't upset that the child didn't say 'I love you' to her, she was thrown by his need to make explicit a public declaration of allegiance to his small nuclear unit by proclaiming "I don't love you". Who's in, who's out. Grandmother, however beloved, is out.

When my daughter-in-law was in hospital, I moved in to be with the children. When she returned she said, "thanks for watching my kids". Watching the children is what the neighbours do – or used to do – while you duck out to the shops for milk. Caring for children for a fortnight is not 'watching'. It is the doing of parenting and the privilege of grandparenting. They are not her children. They are ours. The nuclear option of possessiveness makes them her property, legally, psychically and linguistically. She claims it takes a village. She is blind to the reality that in the village the central power is not hers.

This is what my friend Laura and I understood when I said, 'they want us dead'. Impatient adult sibling daughters want the power that rightfully rests with their mothers. They know there is a place in themselves they cannot reach until we, their ageing mothers, vacate our living bodies on the Earth. In attempting to claim the crown they believe is rightfully theirs before their time, the adult daughters of ageing mothers in modern nuclear families carve fissures through the family structure. In doing so, they snatch too early a status for which they are neither prepared nor equipped. In doing so, they sideline the ageing mother, corralling her off from heart and hearth, fracturing her authority, liquidating her wisdom and rendering her useful not included. I hear my friend Anita's clipped voice saying, "noted, Olivia". She is referencing her adult daughter's tendency to limit her speech and constrain her to this idea or that expression, not-free to speak what the condemnatory adult daughter finds (fill in the fault). For the ageing mother of adults it is a guessing game, one she cannot win. You can be here. You can say this. And be here. And say that. But not there. And not that. Noted, Olivia.

The shifting of the grandmothers from the centre of the modern nuclear family web typifies the distinctive experiences between ageing mothers of adults raised in modern nuclear families and ageing mothers of adults raised in clanned families. In modern nuclear families the status of the ageing mother declines with the birthing of each new generation. She might be rolled out for family photos to showcase the longevity of the line; they may show up for birthdays ending in zero. Ask her, and she will tell you what it is like to watch the sibling children she raised destroy their young, her beloved grandchildren. She is 'allowed' to 'watch' them, to mind them, to be with them in service to the sibling adults she birthed and their partners. She has no power, no authority and little opportunity to offer guidance resultant from the additional decades she has spent navigating the actualities of life on Earth, rather than manufactured social media and television-driven sibling fantasies of how life should be on Earth according to the self-centred needs of one individual.

In the modern western nuclear family, the ageing mother is progressively shifted to the edge of the modern nuclear family line with the birth of each new generation. *Line.* The progression is linear, purposeful. Her invisibility fades quickly until, no longer useful, she registers as an indistinct blip on the family radar. In the clanned family, the ageing mother sustains her place at the centre of the family relational web until she vanishes into the whole, and the mantle at the centre is filled by the next generation.

There is every possibility, and even likelihood, that this representation of the status of the clanned mother has romanticised the status of ageing women in kinship groups, clans and tribes, although it may be fair representation of the domestic and familial power centres. Even so, it stands as observationally true for the clanned families visible to and experienced by this author, specifically among the clanned ageing mothers of adults from Mediterranean, Middle Eastern and Indigenous Australian cultures. These experiential observations are backed by Simone de Beauvoir, who stated: "Strong societies will look to the ageing for support (valuing their memory and experience). In divided societies and in troubled times, the young will take command."

The reader would be in error to transpose or romanticise the status of ageing and elderly people across time and culture. It is not uncommon for industrialised westerners to sentimentalise the 'noble deaths' of the elderly in tribal cultures. In sublime example, I was sitting around the dinner table with a group of (white, western) women. Our discussion turned to the status of ageing women in our society (e.g., varying versions of 'ignored', 'invisible', 'not valued'). One woman narrated the following story: "I was watching a documentary the other night about the Inuit people, how the elderly know when it is their time to die. So they put the old one on the back of a canoe and row her out into the icy water. At some point on the journey she will tip herself off the back of the canoe into the water." The women around the table nodded sagely at such noble death. I roared with laughter.

There is a multitude of wrongs in this story, including the un-examined privilege of the documentary maker to make celluloid myth of geronticide; the absence of consideration by my friends for the agency of the old one; the failure across cultures and through time of societies to care for the no-longer-useful elderly; basic scru-tinisation of whether or not the tale is true. The story is reminiscent of the catchcry of the ageing and elderly in our times, here at the quartermark of the twenty-first century: "I don't want to be a burden to my children." This is how the ageing and elderly disappear them-selves in modern industrialised western economies, reinforcing the self-centredness of the horizontal sibling society and annulling their responsibilities to the vertical, thereby robbing younger generations of the privilege of participation in the return cycle of care in the form of undiminishing respect for the ageing and elderly in their line and the vanishing web.

Simone de Beauvoir put considerable effort into historical cross-cultural examination of realities for the ageing and elderly through time, finding that, with exceptions, the ageing and elderly have not fared particularly well. Rather, outcomes for the ageing and elderly are a chance determination, contingent upon the wealth of the family and society, the culturally-determined status of the ageing and elderly in families and societies, and, in the west, the economic poverty of the individual. In other words, cultural and familial potluck and, in the individualised society, eighty-year-old women who 'made their choices' and are responsible for generating their own resources, finan-cially and otherwise, regardless of the financial status of her adult children.

Many years ago I was watching Australia's at that time ground-breaking multicultural television channel, SBS. There was a brief *vox populi* (that curious media practice of asking random strangers a question). The question in this particular vox pop, undertaken on a busy city street, was this: 'Would you care for your parents if they were sick?' I was young. I wasn't particularly interested – until I noticed stark distinctions in the responses of the strangers. The white people like me said varying versions of 'yes, of course I would, I'd make sure they were put in a home with people to care for them'. The people with olive and darker skins, male and female, said varying versions of 'yes of course. I would stop work and take care of them'. I have no idea why that stuck with me when I was young and steeped in self-focused sibling culture. I do know why I remember it now. It is the difference between a family of thirty-two people and a family of three, often with one adult at the helm. It is the difference between sustaining one's place as central to the family web and being shuffled off into oblivion by sibling adults who claim too young the power centre that is not theirs to claim. I am reminded of the Greek word *hubris*, the most wonderful definition of which was offered by mythologist Patrick Garner: "Hubris is taking the gods' portion for oneself."

Ours is a hubristic society. Well might we ask what price the gods will exact for our individualised sibling conceits. *You think you're so wise.* Yes I think I'm so wise. As you raise your arm to cast that pebble in life's pond, I have the crows' nest advantage of remembrance and experience to see where it will land. I know its trajectory. I can foresee the ripples circling out. In the modern nuclear family I am helpless to stop you, and I cannot protect the children. This is what the refusal of siblings to await their time at the family centre means – not just for their lives, for everyone's lives. Don't take my word for it. It's written in your grandmother's eyes. Peel your sibling gaze from your reflection in the eyes and ways of your horizontal peers, and look up, if you dare, and down, if you will. Your refusal is writ large across the lives of the children, the ageing, the elderly and the ancestors.

The surrender of individuals to kinship groups is not a phenomenon unknown to individualised westerners. Author and former soldier Sebastian Junger posed the following questions: How do you become an adult in a society that doesn't ask for sacrifice? How do you become an (adult) in a world that doesn't require courage? Junger observed that it was not uncommon for white soldiers and civilians kidnapped by First Nations American tribes way back when to refuse to leave the tribe, whilst the reverse was rare. Both questions and observation address the same phenomenon: Adler's community feeling versus private logic. Belonging versus nuclear family disaster.

The tragedy of our fractured family age is emblazoned across the lives of the extraordinary number of western and westernised humans who now live alone, and intensified by the numbers who die without notice. In the first half of 2024 in Japan, more than 37,000 people died alone at home. More than seventy percent were older than sixty-five and it took more than a month to discover almost four thousand of them. The headlines scream 'Japan has a lonely death crisis', as if Japan is an outlier in a universe of modern industrialised westernised living.

This is of course the lament of an ageing woman. At no previous point in my life would I have viewed my aloneness as a tragedy. Now I have raised sibling children and contributed to the raising of sibling grandchildren, and it is me and not my mother, my grandmother and my great grandmother standing at the proverbial gate alone staring at their backs, now it is me who is positioned to interpret the loss and anguish in my mother's eyes – now it is me, I can say: "I see the tragedy." And not just for the ageing and elderly, for the children too, who must live entire childhoods with the catastrophe of the intensifying needs of their sibling parents for 'space' and 'me time', the tragedy being our collective failure to recognise the tragedy. A child I knew when he was eight was obsessed with his screen. I asked him why he didn't put it down and play with someone or talk to someone. His mother perhaps, or his father, or his brother, all of whom, by the way, were staring at screens. He said, "because no-one will play with me". Three years later the same child drove a long distance with an aunt. I asked if it was a screen-free drive, knowing the aunt had been anti-screen. No, he said, explaining the screen was important "so I wouldn't be annoying".

Individualised westerners and others in westernised and westernising nations are losing their capacity to be around other humans. We are burdened by each other. We do not use 'the right words'. We do not use 'the right tone'. We fail to respond in 'the right way'. Mytrauma and myanxiety and myadhd cannot cope with people and situations not framed according to myneeds. This is sibling madness. It cannot be dissociated from a concept well-known to clanned families, and is illusory at best to the unclanned modern nuclear family: loyalty. Family loyalty. In clanned families loyalty is not only a requirement, it is a code. Clanned families know, for better and for worse, that family comes first. The marrying-in to the clanned family are accountable to the standards set by the family. They are answerable to the vertical, up and down the line. There is no 'my' code in the clanned family.

The transfer of loyalty from family to individual others, as is the case in unclanned families, is a silent splintering. It is the place where unpartnered and untethered women become excruciatingly vulnerable, for there is neither vertical nor horizontal gaze looking out for them. There is no witness to the ill-behaviour of others in the family sphere, for loyalty is located elsewhere. Mine is a generation of women who rejected 'outdated' ideas about single women. We campaigned against archaic words such as 'spinster' and decried pity for the unmarried woman. I now understand what all of human history until recently has understood – the world is unkind to unpartnered, untethered women, a reality that sharpens with age like an obsidian blade. The Russian writer Fyodor Dostoevsky, in addressing the self-centredness of modern individuals, might say that if you want to know about the ills in a society look at the relationships in the families that make up that society. Individualised families loyal to the horizontal gaze cannot be well families. They are looking only at themselves. Their guiding inputs come from broken peers and ad men. Modern industrialised nuclear families must face what the ancients knew all along, and the clanned still know – strong families are loyal families and that loyalty ultimately rests with the elders to make decisions for the clan.

Vertical, not horizontal.

Several years ago, in a wellbeing writing workshop I was facilitating in a regional town on the fringe of outback Australia, a social worker struggled to write. On exploration, she briefly shared with the group the unhappiness in her isolated nuclear family: a recent divorce, a violent ex-husband, three troubled and unhappy children, her despair. She said, "I visit Indigenous families for work. Their yards are full of broken toys. There are kids everywhere. The house is over-crowded with people. And I look at my beautiful house. And my children's perfect toys. And the Aboriginal kids are so happy and my kids are miserable and I'm thinking 'why am I supposed to be making you more like us'?"

The social worker is not romanticising structural poverty. Rather, she is comprehending and coming to terms with the sentimentalised fiction of the nuclear disaster that is her own fractured family. Broadcast philosopher Waleed Ali observed: "You can't spin a culture out of individualism." The same can be said for families. Siblings raised by siblings, whose primary loyalty is to themselves, cannot create strong kinship groups, let alone a society in which the children, the ageing, the elderly and even the sibling-raised want to live. Thus in meeting the second of our contemporary monsters, the modern nuclear family, we are positioned to observe how the first, individualism, is birthed in, thrives on and feeds the nuclear disaster that is the privatised, isolated, fractured modern western industrialised family. This, in cyclical and sibling-predictable turn, has given rise to the third contemporary monster: the mental health industry.

## The rise and rise of industrialised mental health

The ascendancy of industrialised mental health is individualism's finest hour. Many things, in this instance two, can be true at once: we live in challenging times: war, plague, climatic disaster, planetary crisis; we live at a time when life has never been more comfortable for such a critical number of people. In the non-indigenous west and the elite elsewhere we are more at risk of death from overeating than starvation, from suicide than war. Almost all of us have shelter and running hot water. We travel at whim. Our offspring need nothing, want for nothing, have everything yet are beset by 'mental health issues'. We in the west have everything. Not in the sense that individual persons and families have everything a person or family could need or want, although that too. Rather, we believe it is our collective right to possess *everything*. All the water. All the minerals. All the technology. All the toys. All the food. All the pretty dresses. All the clean air. All the weapons. All the land. Everything.

Two words: mental, health. Strung together they are in our times a powerful little axiom established as fact. Industrialised mental health is one of the fastest growing industry sectors in western nations. What is this gobbler of national and international budgetary resources? Where is the evidence that our collective mental health is improving with the gargantuan sums of money funnelling into the private bank accounts of the experts? What is the influence of the mental health industry on our society? How does the industrialised language of the scientists and experts shape the language, behaviour, identities, health, wellbeing and lifestyles of individuals, families and communities? What is the impact of industrialised mental health on individuals, families and communities? Is the rise and rise of the mental health industry connected to the fall and failure of western, westernised and westernising families? Is there any such thing as 'mental health'? Can 'mental health' be separated from the physical body that does the living? Is psychology the new church? These questions are neither idle nor ideological, for just as the modern nuclear family is unsustainable, so too is the current 'mental health crisis'. Either we're all going under, or we take a good hard look at the language and publicly-funded lifestyles of the experts, and examine for ourselves the veracity and voracity of the doctrines to which we-who-have-everything submit ourselves and our children. This chapter addresses these questions through texts and ideas abandoned by the wayside of the century-long march towards the pontifical dominance of industrialised psychology in our world.

In street parlance, for the purposes of this book, the cornerstones of industrialised mental health are threefold: mental health, psychology/psychiatry and neuroscience. Mental health, as the term is widely understood at this time, pertains to the health and wellbeing of the mental realm, the mind. Psychology is, strictly speaking, the study of human thought and behaviour. Psychiatry is the medicalisation of psychology/mental health. Neuroscience focuses on the biological mechanisms of thinking, feeling and doing. The co-relationship between mental health and psychology/psychiatry is the locus of our explorations of this contemporary monster.

The concept 'mental health' was initially languaged as 'mental hygiene' by psychiatry in the mid-1800s. From the 1920s into the post-war 1940s, 'mental illness' became the preferred term. By the 1960s mental illness was repackaged by the Americans as 'mental health', shifting the focus of specialists from severe emotional, behavioural and 'abnormal' disorders (with profound acknowledgement for the non-conforming women ensnared in this net) to the disorder-making of life itself, a repositioning that empowered and sanctioned the ascendancy of a chimera beloved and sanctioned by the sibling society: 'my inner self'. Thus 'mental health' has become the current populist catch-all for matters mental, emotional, behavioural and therapistic, and in common parlance is applied interchangeably with 'psychological'.

Psychology's remit is the development of theories to explain human thought and behaviour. This has led to the development of strategies to 'fix' apparently errant thoughts and behaviour – often via the same experiments and research created to test the idea that underpinned the research in the first place (snake, tail). For that is what a theory is: an idea. An idea is a hunch, a speculation, an opinion. A theory is a thought bubble given meaning by pattern-making, naming and a good marketing strategy. In the beginning – as with all industries there was a beginning – these ideas were formulated in the minds of clever young men of means, and developed in conjunction with other clever young men of means, means enough to sit in European coffee houses and ruminate, argue, debate and reinforce each other's brilliance whilst their lesser caste peers broke their backs working machinery, sweeping chimneys and going to war(s). In other words, mental health as we know it is an idea developed by a select group of elite young men from a particular time, place and culture that has come to exert outsized influence on the lives of women, children, families and communities not of their time, place or culture, in the process making their transformational way from theory to unquestioned, dogmatic 'reality'.

Is mental health real?

Questioning whether mental health is real in our times is akin to questioning the reality of God in medieval England. Unlike atoms and microbes awaiting scientific discovery with microscopes and other paraphernalia, and quantum physics with its capability for venturing into yet-unimagined universes, it is entirely possible that, despite the psychology sector's nearly two centuries-long attempt to be recognised as a legitimate science, no entity called 'mental health' exists, let alone is awaiting discovery. The maligned psychiatric theorist Thomas Szasz considered 'mental disease' a *metaphor* for troubling behaviours, thoughts or social nonconformity, and cautioned against literal interpretations of belief systems that medicalise or demonise human difference. He stated, "mental illness is a myth, whose function is to disguise and thus render more palatable the bitter pill of moral conflicts in human relations". Szasz challenged assumptions about norms of 'good human behaviour', deviation from which is a sure sign of 'mental disorder'. Concerned about the direction psychiatry was taking in the 1960s, he identified three logical pathways for interrogating, assessing, describing and redressing industrialised efforts to isolate 'mental health' from the act of living in a body. The pathways are:

(a)  neurological, that is, of the brain
(b)  deviation from a pre-set social, ethical or legal 'normal'
(c)  a living-in-the-world problem.

The son of a neighbour, for example. Let's call him called Peter. Peter's mother speaks of 'Peter's anxiety' as if this behavioural state is as much a part of Peter as an arm, a leg or an entity with a life of its own, such as a beloved pet that needs regular feeding. It is as if 'Peter's anxiety' is a statement of fact, a structural identity, a concrete noun, a *reality*. A while back I caught up with Peter. He mentioned he was taking ADHD drugs. When he was a child Peter's aunt had taught him to breathe his way through panic and discipline his attention through a martial art. When he mentioned he was taking ADHD drugs I asked him why he didn't go to judo. He replied: "Why would I when I can take a pill?"

Why would he, indeed.

Here's the other thing about Peter. He was an unusual child. He was outrageously funny. He was provocative. He was incisively clever, engaging and witty. He was spontaneous and original. With the pills the world has won. Peter is socially normalised. No longer as funny. Not as bright. Not as engaging. Rude in a whole new way, the cookie-cutter sibling society way.

What modern psychology/psychiatry has diagnosed as Peter's mental health problems can be reconstructed via Szasz in the following ways:

(a)  neurological – the ADHD drugs don't work on Peter's 'mental health', they work on the physical matter that is his brain
(b)  a demand for social normativity – Peter's behaviour now fits an arbitrarily defined social 'norm'; he is acceptable, he is 'normal'
(c)  a living-in-the-world problem – Peter is unwilling to square up to lifeworld challenges and take action on his own behalf (e.g., commit to a focused discipline such as a martial art), preferring instead to take a pill.

Until Peter is willing to act on his own behalf to master his feeling responses to life, his anxiety-now-ADHD will be his to have and to hold for the rest of his life, or until the budgetary generosity of his government runs out. *He is that.* For if we question the premise that mental health is real, and we accept that Peter has a living in the world problem, then we must also query whether all the money and all the therapy in the world is going to fix the 'mental health crisis' when its partakers prefer to take a pill. And if we follow this path to its logical conclusion, we may reach an explanation for why, despite the budgetary billions thrown at 'mental health' each year, the mental health of individuals in western societies is in catastrophic decline. Drugs work on Peter's physical body; they normalise his behaviour and his personality; they relieve him from responsibility for managing 'his' anxiety and ADHD. Talk therapy – modern psychology – has replaced friendship in the modern industrialised west. Most of Peter's friends are digital. He may have met them at some point, but given the international nature of his friendship base they are virtual entities, avatars, eidolons, disembodied phantoms with whom he need not leave his room to engage.

Peter is a lonely young man who sees a therapist and takes a pill. Peter's therapist will likely be sibling-raised and sibling-educated, a sibling expert uncooked in the firepits of life. S/he may be no older than Peter himself. Talk therapy – modern psychology – is poor replacement for clan guidance; that is, engagement with the expectancies and limitations imposed by the elders, and the requisite return-cycle of loyalty, respect, goodwill and standards that are critical to the sustenance of family and clan, and, for that matter, the health and wellbeing of individuals. 'Why would I when I can take a pill' can be readily substituted for 'why would I listen to them (elders/clan) when I can pay someone to whom I owe nothing, who will listen to everything I say and who can realistically expect nothing (therapist)'. Peter's 'diagnosis' has provided him with a perpetual alibi for disengagement from self, clan and the world on any other than his own too-young-to-determine terms. He is of the genera-tion that wants for nothing. Like much of his individualised western nuclear family-raised generation, he's a 'nice guy' and an indulged adult. He is unbeholden to clan. He is a man with a lazy spine and a sibling-selfish heart who is absolved from taking action on his own behalf.

As is the daughter of a friend, who is about Peter's age. My friend's daughter recently visited a family friend, a practicing psychiatrist, seeking an ADHD diagnosis. He obliged. Said my friend: "She is so relieved to have a diagnosis for why she is different." Please don't ask me to spell out all the things wrong with this story. Further to this, at the time of writing I am horrified by the number of middle aged and agcing women self-diagnosing – and then proudly broadcasting – 'their' ADHD diagnosis. Last year's mental health trend was 'on the spectrum'. The year before that it was 'mytrauma'. We are heading into a period of self-proclaimed 'neurodivergence'. Surely this is sibling-adult madness, whereby each member of the sibling society has their own individualised mental health diagnosis with its own language and its own needs, requiring others to play the mercurial guessing game of what your mytrauma requires, insists upon, needs from other people today. It appears we are so desperate for absolution from the actuality that real-life can be Sisyphus-hard that we are determined to seek diagnosis; and that we are so diminished in our capacity as adults we cannot ignore the siren call to distraction and at the very least put down the phone, thereby giving ourselves half a chance at restoring calm, focus and productive pursuit to our lives.

Diagnostic trends are theories. They exist because people say they exist. For those clamouring for a diagnosis to explain why they are 'different' I have good news – when everyone is on the spectrum and everyone has ADHD you're not different. You're just like all the others. You cannot have it both ways – you're either different or you're the same. And you cannot 'fix' something that does not exist. You can numb yourself from it. You can tell yourself a story that absolves you from what living asks from you. You can join the ranks of the self-proclaimed broken so you too can be exceptional(ly the same). But you cannot fix something that is an idea, a theory, a thought bubble with a marketing plan. You cannot fix something that doesn't exist, and I prefer this theory – the one that does not distinguish mental health from health (i.e., the enspirited health of a body with breath in it). I prefer the story that prioritises community feeling ahead of private logic and the bottomless well of a mental diagnosis for everyone.

---

*This is particularly so when there are people in our community who really truly absolutely do need public resources to help out and put life on an even keel. The drain of the worried well and the already-have-everything is liquidating the capacity of people with acute needs to receive the professional help and resources they urgently need.*

---

If we turn our backs on the dual logic of the theoreticians, that pain is physical and suffering is emotional, we are positioned to accept Szasz's premise there is no such thing as mental health in isolation from the body and the world. If this is so, then we must also accept that Peter, my friend's daughter and a great swathe of the missing-out middle aged do not have a mental health problem. They have a living-in-the-world problem. They are humans hiding behind a diagnosis. They are the worried well. So whilst we can dispute the existence of mental health as a tangible entity, we cannot dispute, unless we're being too clever by half, the existence of the body. Trauma specialist Peter Levine addressed the inadequacy of "therapeutic approaches that neglect the body" and could not be clearer about the body's central place in addressing human health and wellbeing:

> "Since the body enacts survival options (alert, flight, fright, freeze, fold) it is the body's narration that must (be) addressed … in transforming trauma."

Whilst I have no idea about Levine's response to, or attitudes towards, 'mental health', I do know he wrote an entire book on trauma without once mentioning 'mental health'. He placed the term "mental disorders" in inverted commas, and rarely mentioned 'psychological' in relation to trauma except regarding the work of psychologists and psychiatrists. For Levine, the primary fodder of the mental health industry – shame, blame, anxiety, paralysis, fear, catatonia, rage, numbness, hopelessness – takes place in the body. All of it, in the body. So it is the body to which Levine has turned his attention in en/countering trauma in the people with whom he works.

The modern mental health industry has subsumed, converged with and is now inseparable from the populist 'new age' industry and its pseudo-spiritual 'teachings' and vernacular. Consequently, academic theories and rhetoric have infiltrated everyday language and consciousness, including that of children, leaving those of us in the west with no area of our lives free from the impositions of 'mytruth' (our own and/ or others'), 'myneeds', 'mypurpose' and quests for 'myauthenticself'. For decades now we have been at the mercy of these tomb-raiding charlatans promising the treasures of ancient teachings that were once earned through selective processes that demanded significant commitment, time and surrender; teachings that are now available for purchase over a weekend. Trinkets dressed as treasure, they lose their lustre the moment the initiate has returned to the world she hoped to 'transcend'. Such promises have been constructed around the so-called 'inner self'. You know who she is. She is the one proclaiming 'my truth', the one you believe is your inner voice, the one perpetually puzzled by and in pursuit of the 'right path' and 'my true purpose'. This inner self we keep feeding is a monster. No matter how much of ourselves we sacrifice to her wants and ways she is never, ever satisfied.

The inner self is a modern invention and I for one have had enough of her. She's there in all her monstrous guises in every writing program I've ever run, halls of mirrors of the monster within gobbling up all that is good and brave about the writer seeking her voice. The inner self is a liar. She's a wrecking ball. She's a riot. She's a thief. She creates illusions of 'truth'. She makes trouble. All this in the name of 'mental health' and 'spiritual evolution'. I see her in the writing circles, there and there and there and there, telling spirited women they are too stupid to write a book, too foolish to want to try, too unworthy, too big for her boots, a failure and no-one wants to read what she has to say anyway. All the prisms of time-wasting personal assault a human woman can muster to trash what her psyche most longs for: to write herself into the world, self made matter on the page, visible as she knows herself to be. An entire industry has been founded in honour of this illusion. We have handed the charlatans the keys to our kingdom.

This 'inner self' did not exist a hundred years ago. It is a product, a fabrication whose development is credited to Sigmund Freud, and like much else in western thought since the age of reason, including 'mental health', it is an idea that has been isolated, separated, segregated, packaged and brought to market. Humans for almost all of human history did not have to deal with their 'inner self', which is not the same as intuition or gut instinct, and has nothing at all to do with soul/psyche as per the original meaning of the word. In our times there is a 'health' for anyone ready to 'discover' a 'disorder', become an expert, build a career and forge an industry out of their theories and imaginings. So deeply embedded are these ideas in our culture, so completely have we adopted them, we are no longer able to distinguish 'reality' from what they are and always were: theory. And theories, as researcher Jill Astbury observes, are "powerful ideological instruments in the creation of neurosis".

Neurosis is a term historically associated with women. It is women who were and are 'neurotic', with their tendencies towards hysteria, emotional excess and nervous disorders. The mental health industry has a long history of convincing women they are suffering malady and madness. It's not surprising then that men have traditionally been slow on the uptake of products and services on offer, given they were never the intended targets and are in fact the norm against which the 'mental health' of women and children is measured. That modern western society is driving them no less 'mad' is another matter.

In coining the phrase 'neurotic science', the nineteenth century diarist Alice James flipped the lens onto the theorists, prompting Jill Astbury to observe that the development of theories of neurosis says "infinitely more about the observer than the observed". Whilst this is not a book about women and madness, it nonetheless behoves us to remember two things: firstly, women were formally excluded from the elite educational institutions that developed the cornucopia of theories about them; and secondly, that women have every right to be enraged, aka 'neurotic', about their pre-determined status in society and their treatment by and the impositions of men in power. The millennia-long exclusion of women from formal education ceded wide territory for clever, wealthy young men to pontificate, deliberate, ponder, discuss and pronounce upon the mental states, capacities, capabilities and right use of women. In the process they developed what Astbury described as "ideological concepts and malignant fantasies of woman (which) for too long masqueraded as neutral descriptions of her nature". In doing so, they composed "complicated solutions to what the researchers themselves had constructed as the problem".

The pathologisation of women runs direct to source through time to those weighty Athenian philosophers who, like the gurus of the new age, corrupted the teachings of the time before them. In the words of philosopher Peter Kingsley, the Athenians turned from philosophy as love of wisdom to philosophy as "the love of talking and arguing about the love of wisdom". The history of hysteria can be traced to these men, who were resolute in their theory that hysteria was caused by a wandering uterus, the salve for which was and is marriage in order to summon the uterine pilgrim to its rightful place.

Scholar Maria Massucco tells us Freud updated the wandering uterus theory, the remedy for which was heterosexual sex and pregnancy to "root that uterus back where it belongs". Massucco points out that once Freud understood the extent of sexual abuse endured by women in wealthy families, he generalised the needs and experiences of his clients rather than addressing the issue itself. For psychoanalysis to be accepted as legitimate practice it required the assent of the wealthy elite. Freud, unwilling to risk scandal, diverted attention from where the true problem lay, that is, with men sexually using and abusing women, and instead concocted sweeping diagnoses of female hysteria. Career, profit, licence to practice. Strange that the startlingly obvious – women's position in society – might not be justification enough for her 'errant' behaviour. Clearly women had and have a living in the world problem.

Another debunked theory concocted by industrialised mental health, which also targeted women, was 'multiple personality disorder'. This theory fractured lives, devastated families and cost practitioners millions in payouts in the United States. And yet today we have the same theory redistributed amongst other predominantly female disorders and its central premise repackaged as 'dissociative identity disorder'. This is despite cautionary counsel thirty years ago by the director of psychiatry at John Hopkins University, Paul McHugh: "In but a few years, we will all look back (on the 'multiple personality disorder' movement) and be dumbfounded by the gullibility of the public in the late twentieth century and by the power of psychiatric assertions to dissolve common sense."

It seems we have a long way to go.

Towards the end of that same century, Jill Astbury observed that "we continue to know more about what the scientific experts think of women's nature and what is needed for the 'normal' functioning of their lives than we do about what women think about themselves and believe might be for their own good". It is not news to women or the world that men have constructed women in their own interests. Compliance and conformity are 'normal'. To deviate is to be 'abnormal'. If women were a nation it would long ago have been recognised we are under assault and at war, regardless of whether we are fighting for our lives (abnormal) or compliant (normal). The words of the

Russo-American revolutionary Emma Goldman come to mind: "As a woman I have no country. As a woman, my country is the whole world."

The inclusion of women in the psychological sciences over recent decades has left women to pick up these threads at their point of entry into corporate universities. They are primarily young women, unschooled in the unchallenged nature of the theories that comprise the knowledge base that informs their training. The mental health industry is imbued with the inequalities and stereotypes of all the spheres of influence in a woman's life: cultural, social, economic, political, domestic, geographical. The two-century-long march of the mental health industry, constructing theories built on theories built on theories masking gender, class and race determinants of who has the problem and who gets to decide, has concocted the very 'mental health' problems it now attempts to solve. If your therapist cannot articulate the foundational ideas that frame, drive and infuse her work then her work amounts to brainwashing and is counter to your interests.

The problem with the western mind *is* the western mind. Says Kingsley: "We create schemes and structures and climb up and down inside them. But these are just monkey tricks and parlour games to console us and distract us from the longing in our hearts." In sublime complexity, for readers seeking intricate support for this statement, academic David Bates penned the following:

> "What we mean by the mind is the continuing and always failing attempt to bring unity to the multiple systems in play. As such, the mind is not itself a unity with given norms and therefore an object of scientific study, but instead an evolving contingent effort to capture the varying logics of survival that stem from our biological, socio-political and technical systems. The mind is both defined by these systems and is resolutely not these systems."

*The continuing and always failing attempt to bring unity to the multiple systems in play.* In other words, the thinking that created diagnoses endemic to modern western societies cannot possibly generate solutions to those same problems (snake, tail). Monkey tricks and parlour games may offer distraction and consolation to the mind defined by the systems it created. However, even though the mind may be defined by those systems, *it is resolutely not these systems.*

Psychotherapist Thomas More beseeches us to read the poets before the psychologists, cautioning that to neglect the soul is to "lose our humanity and our individuality". Enter poet Amanda Gorman, who addressed what the scientists call 'stereotypic' behaviour in mammals, that is, 'repetitive and unvarying actions such as incessant pacing, over-grooming, rocking, kicking, excessive sleeping and self mutilation'. Gorman points out that stereotypic behaviour is unknown in the wild, that "it is considered a strong indicator of poor psychological health in the caged organism". Whilst stereotypic is considered 'abnormal', Gorman asks the question: is it the animal demonstrating such behaviour that is 'abnormal' or the conditions society has imposed upon its living? Which in turn lends itself to the central thesis of this particular contemporary monster – that 'mental health' cannot be isolated from the conditions of the body doing the living.

If we accept the west does not have a mental health crisis but a health crisis, a crisis that is deeply connected to soul/psyche and the social and domestic conditions in which it makes its way in the world, then salutogenically it is imperative we turn our attention away from the 'mental health' of individualised humans (i.e., 'Peter's anxiety') to the body that lives in the constructed world in which those same individuals do their living. Salutogenesis and wellbeing-as-assembled, rooted in the phenomenology of living, designate health and wellbeing as beyond the auspice of individuals. Rather, through these lenses, health is viewed as an assemblage of the social, political, economic, domestic and geographical conditions in which human beings live. For example, if the Palestinian woman whose thirty-two family members perished in the Israel Defence Forces' obliteration of her people were to suffer 'mental health issues', is the problem 'her' mental health or might it have been the near-globally-sanctioned war on her people? Is it possible to 'fix' the 'mental health' of individuals being bombed and starved into oblivion without addressing the conditions of their living? Is it possible to fix the 'mental health' of individual prisoners in a prison reliant on isolationist policies of rolling lockdowns when the problem is understaffing of the prison? Is it possible to fix 'Peter's mental health' when Peter himself would prefer to take a pill? Without a shadow of doubt people need support for their health and wellbeing during challenging times, however their mental health cannot be separated from, in this instance, the bombs that destroy their homes, the blockades that prohibit the entry of aid, the politics of cruelty that denies them food and murders their children. There is no mental health without the health of the body, and whilst that in itself is no guarantee of mental health, we might consider it a good start.

The diagnoses, pronouncements, announcements and claims developed by industrialised mental health have no independent existence. They are not lifeforms; they are not a cat or a bee or a flower of recognisable tangibility. They are inflictions; behavioural, emotional, cultural and even moral responses collated, identified and named in keeping with the subjective projections, social prejudices, expectations, trends and standards of the times, thereby framing the human experiences of individuals, families and communities inside the domestic, political, cultural, industrial, economic conditions of the world inside which we play out our lives. In other words, they do not exist by themselves. They are ideas run riot. They are not real. They are theories made up, manufactured and marketed. They are health and wellbeing challenges rooted in systemic values that shape the conditions of our living. And after all this, the sad fact is the mental health industry has no meaningful language for our living.

Further, the industrialised focus on mental health as of individual concern exonerates governments and policy makers from the policies and practices they impose on families, communities and nations. It is easier to fund a war *and* a mental health crisis, both of which channel voluminous public funds into private pockets, than it is to address the crisis of western living in a world constructed to give us everything we want whilst simultaneously destroying the soul on the inside. The idea that we can address systemic problems for individuals without addressing the systemic conditions in which those same problems were generated is symptomatic of the core problem. *The problem with the western mind is the western mind.* Money has not fixed the mental health crisis. Therapy has not fixed the mental health crisis. Pharmaceuticals have not fixed the mental health crisis. Addressing the 'mental health' needs of individuals as if it is 'their' depression, anxiety, ADHD and so on has not fixed the mental health crisis.

Perhaps the nastiest twist in mental health's industrialised tale is the collective rounding on 'mother', as if the entirety of an individual's woes can be traced to one living woman disconnected from the economic, political, social and domestic mores, laws, fads and circumstances of her time. 'Mother' is where the convergence of the mental health sector and the selectively abstractive nature of the new age industry comes of age. The psyche/soul seeks maturity, which necessitates commitment, instruction and the discipline of self. Conversely, the 'inner self' in ascendancy, fuelled by blithe and poorly constituted mental health and new age commentary, hungers for abrogation from responsibility. Freud's contemporary Alfred Adler addressed this ingenuous wraith directly, observing that an individual who seeks justification for her failure to act on her own behalf will "twist and turn and distort" experience until it fits her exalted story of herself. In this way she will find an "effective alibi for as long as (s)he wishes it so"; and, regardless of her excuses, she "betrays one thing, and that is (s)he wishes to be excused from further responsibility".

Thus populist mental health and analysis found a ready consumer market in an individualistic society looking for quick fixes and straw women to reproach for their failings. Blaming 'mother' for who she was, who she was not, who she should have been, who she could have been, what she should have done, could have done, did do, did not do, and so on is the easy out. In other words, in this most vicious assessment, mother could not win. After all, we know what mothers are like.

In what may have been a shot across the bow to Freud and his followers, Adler issued therapists a "responsibility to caution", urging them to exhaustive examination and care before letting loose their theories in the world:

> "The science of human nature may not be approached with too much presumption and pride. On the contrary, its understanding stamps those who practice it with a certain modesty. It is a science that cannot be pursued with the sole purpose of developing occasional experts. Only the understanding by every human being can be its proper goal. This is a sore point with academic investigators who consider their research is the exclusive property of a scientific group."

He went further, cautioning against "the unthinking enthusiasm of young explorers" in psychology, who are without the advantage of having lived through psychic crises. Therapists, he observed, must have capacity for having "the whole in view" before drawing conclusions. This they cannot do when reliant on psychology by numbers, that is, statistics, the preeminent data source for modern psychological education and investigation.

Adler, writing in the early 1900s, argued that families were prone to isolation, and that connection to clan and community was vital to understanding human nature. This idea is supported by historian Dan Edelstein, who tells us individualism is the distortion of the concept of 'natural law'. From the ancient Greeks through to influential political theorists of the sixteenth and seventeenth centuries such as Hobbes and Locke, and onwards to today, natural law offered elements of reprieve and licence to individuals whose lives were and are burrowed inside overbearing political systems. However, whilst 'natural law' once constituted an essential universal moral component, in the age of rampant individualism beset with 'my' 'rights' we have inherited natural law minus the legitimising aegis of 'our' and 'we'. Natural law, the genesis of what we know as 'human rights', is now bereft of its fundamental tenet: that it be universally true for all beings. Therefore, and I sincerely hope I'm stating the obvious, the very conditions for genuinely understanding mental health and psychology are absent from the modern western world. Indeed, the modern west has laid the foundations for the very crisis it seeks to avert.

For almost everyone, what we term 'mental health' is at root symptomatic of a society swamped by a crisis of shaming, exile and the absence of belonging. To return to our friend Peter as an example. Peter may well have a living the world problem, however through this lens the problem is not 'Peter's' but symptomatic of the world we have collectively constructed and our children are inheriting, a world in which the individual reigns supreme unbeholden to that same collective, a world of individuals seeking legitimacy for undisciplined behaviours. To call on Adler once more, all therapy must be of benefit not to the individual but to society. Therefore the question is not, 'what' will we do about it? The question is, 'are we willing' to do anything about it? For make no mistake, genuine willingness will ask something from us, and that something will require surrender of what we 'want' and what we think we 'deserve' and what we say is 'mine by right'. Indeed, it may ask everything we know about the world in return for the genuine restoration of health and wellbeing in the west, and consequently, by extension if we can manage it, everywhere else too.

## The omphalos of *lusus naturae*

The entangled trio of contemporary monsters presented in this chapter represents an assembled crisis not of 'mental health', but of unactioned Longing, unmanaged capital L Loneliness and miscomprehended capital L Love. A crisis of unactioned Longing is a calamity of soul/psyche. A crisis of unmanaged Loneliness is a refusal of the invitation to maturity, to self mastery. A crisis of miscomprehended love or Love is perhaps best explained through a current contagion in the modern west – the incessant 'I love you' trailing children every single time they leave the house. The children, lest they upset their sibling mother, mutter the obligatory 'love you too' in return. This, friends, is not love. It is the transmission of panic. It is possession. It is the imposition of adult instability upon children. It is fear of becoming tomorrow's headline: *'At least if you don't make it home I can tell the media the last thing I said was 'I love you'.'* It is rarely uttered by children to anyone outside their personalised nuclear disaster, regardless of the love the children actually feel for non-nucleared others. It is symptomatic of the generation of parents who assert that their parents didn't tell them they loved them (enough). Ironic then, isn't it, that the I-love-you generation of parents waves off their children with one eye, perhaps two, on the phone. Whatever this is, this *lusus naturae,* this disfiguring of the natural order, it is neither love nor Love.

There is an old legend you know well, only you are unlikely to know it as the tale of the thirteenth fairy. You will know it as Sleeping Beauty. The old version of this tale is the legend of the uninvited guest. It is relevant to multitudinal aspects of modern western living, including and most obviously the sibling society's obsessive mythmaking about happiness. When the king and queen of that old kingdom threw a party to celebrate the birth of their daughter, they invited twelve fairies in the land. They welcomed the beautiful fairies with their shining, unchallenging gifts for the princess child; gifts of grace and joy, a musical voice, a serene temperament, and beauty, naturally. They ignored the old crone, weathered and wizened and wild and wise, uninvited and unwelcome at the party, deeply unappealing in allure and demeanour. She is, after all, the one who sees all, and hears everything. She knows your secrets. She knows what you do not speak. She knows what every princess bride-to-be needs to know to make her way in the world. This is her gift. Ignoring her, shunning her gift, will not end well, for anyone. *She is the ageing woman back with redoubled strength.*

Wisdom lies in what's ignored. Wisdom is not retributive. Wisdom hides in death, metaphorical or otherwise. Wisdom is not kind. We in the west run from sacrifice. We flee from challenge. We deny our Longing. And here's the rub – we might outrun just about anything, we cannot outrun the Longing of the human soul/psyche. Reiterated, the soul/psyche is not the inner self. The inner self is the grasping wanter within, the perpetual child, the eternal self-focused sibling. Wanting is the stomping ground of the inner self. Soul is the maturing adult. Psyche is gravitas. Longing is the realm of the soul/psyche. All the drugs and all the therapies and all the distractions in the world will not still the Longing of psyche/soul (well, all the drugs might).

Physicist F. David Peat reminds us that 'the European mind is young and its science is an infant'. Equating the European mind with western consciousness, he observes the expansion, dominance and hubris of the European mind found nirvana in the USA, where all three contemporary monsters relish *sanctum sanctorum* among the white middle classes, wriggling their haunches like cats in long grass, making ready to ingurgitate the world. The children and the ageing and elderly stand ready for not their redemption but yours, the empowered sibling adults that rule our lives, and the faint pulse of unhopeful faith in the triumph of community feeling over private logic.

The unsettling reality is that unactioned, Longing will haunt you until the day you die. Says Kingsley: "The voice of our longing is repetition, insistently calling out to what's beyond anything we're familiar with or even understand." The modern westerner seeking 'true purpose' and 'authenticity' and 'inner truth' will remain dissatisfied and distressed until the day she understands everything she seeks is already right there inside her. *The longing is the path.* The only question is, will you follow your Longing where it leads? Will you follow Longing, knowing there will be no guarantees of 'success' and no promises about 'outcomes', and not ever knowing until you get 'there' what it will ask from you, only to discover this is no 'there'?

Longing will lead you to the edge of your known world. In Parmenides' famous poem it will take you *as far as longing can reach*. And beyond that, well, wisdom lies over the edge. It demands a leap and a price, and that price is your acquisitive inner self. It invites you to the journey of soul/psyche. It asks your sacrifice, your courage, your willingness to visit the dark heart of wisdom, from there to allow the possibility of return, no longer a grasping sibling but a human being matured. This is the wisdom of the thirteenth fairy. When the divine is removed from the depths, as it is in the mental health industry, as it is in the sibling society, as it is in the nuclear disaster of the industrialised modern western family, as it is in an individualised universe of one, we lose our depth. The alternative, says Kingsley, is to "suffer as liabilities and die as statistics".

# 3.

## Slow Burn Exile

IT IS A TIME of great joy. All four of my grandchildren are living along the same arterial road in the same capital city, all four within forty minutes' drive from each other. The eldest, my beloved granddaughter, is eighteen. Her brother is sixteen. Their cousins, my son's children, are seven and one. I am staying with my sixteen-year-old grandson for a couple of months so his mother, my daughter, can holiday. One afternoon my granddaughter messaged me, asking if I'd pick up some toilet paper for her on my way over to visit. Of course I would. Along the way I swung by my son's home to say hello. The traffic was heavy. The local shops would have scant parking. I stood in the living room of my son's home, him at one end of the room, his wife at the other. I asked if I could take a roll of toilet paper over to K. It was a moot question, of course I could.

"No," they said in unison.

I laughed. I thought they were joking.

"I'll return it tomorrow," I said, playing along with the joke.

"No," they said.

The strangest element of this scenario is the unanimity of their response. They are standing five metres apart at either end of a large room. I tell them about the traffic, how I'd rather not try and find a park at the supermarket.

"No," they chorused.

I stood in the centre of the room I could no longer see. My body remained erect yet an internal shell was splintering. I was imploding, possessed by the image of a skyscraper standing tall, its glass internality shattering and crashing to earth while the building itself remained upright. I was winded. I lost my senses. The world itself made no sense. I was no-one. As may be obvious, the omphalos of this ageing mother's body is etched for all time with the shards of this experience. Six weeks later she would mind their baby for a month while they travelled to India, taking the child for a week in the lead-up to their trip to wean him.

It is worth noting the elements of this experience that are visible to the world, namely, the engaged mother and grandmother at the hub of family life. It is also worth noting she is an unpartnered woman. Nothing of this ageing mother and grandmother's experience is known to the world outside her skin. It was a private agony she shared with no-one, until now.

Living with a broken heart is a women's art. Women lose. It's what we do. As we age we lose everything that had value to us and for which we were valued. In a woman-framed world this might be cause for celebration. Simone de Beauvoir lamented the absence of rites of passage for the coming of age (and she didn't mean twenty-one). As it is, it sneaks up on us until, without apparent warning, we find ourselves marooned as the tide of life recedes taking everything with it, leaving us lost and abandoned on the shoreline. Those we have loved and nurtured turn their faces away, and our voices and our visibility fade with the harsh chill of a new reality: we do not exist in their world, not as we know ourselves to be. The voices of the women who arrived in this place before us echo along the shoreline. Oh. We remember. We heard them. When we were young and self-important. We paid them no mind. We turned away. We neither honoured nor vaguely acknowledged her grief, if we recognised it as grief at all. We dismissed her lament unkindly as the passing moan of an old woman unable to bear her irrelevance. We wondered why she did not 'get on with her life', failing utterly to comprehend that, regardless of the trappings of her life, we *were* her life, front and centre. We were wilfully blind. Our failure to share the pain in her heart was and has been and is needless and brutal, our myopic vision clouding what was there to see all along – our face reflected in the slammed door hall of mirrors of women left behind.

Men lose too. The tide of irrelevance will come for them, but much later in life, when they are no longer 'productive'. Women lose when we are at our maximum advantage. We appear to be the only ones who know this, and we do not know it until we've trained our daughters to turn away. Too late. We know they will eventually wash up on this shoreline. We could speak it flat to their faces and they would not hear it. Like ageing eyesight and the face of their great grandmother, they are deaf to the heralding tide.

Alone, we turn to see our island is full of marooned women who have learned to live with the grieving, who have mastered the art of living with a broken heart. Women who are no longer frightened by loss because there is nothing left to lose. Women who know how to roar with laughter. That roar is also a woman's art. Women who nod with ah-yes familiarity for your grief, for we are living a pattern of exile from the tribal heart/h. Exile is an external horror unleashed on the spirit. Estrangement takes root in the bones. The unspoken accountings of women are the threads that weave the cloth that binds the wounds and cloak the living and bury the dead. It has ever been this way, the lost tellings of women, in you and all around you, in your grandmother's watery eyes that speak of longing so great as she waves you off after a rare visit you both know you will not return any time soon.

There is a missing word in the English language, and that is the word for 'adult children'. People who are in their forties and fifties and sixties are not children. Nor are those in their twenties and thirties. For the record, young adults, those in their late teens, are not 'children' either. All of them are 'offspring', but offspring are not necessarily adults. I am the mother of adult children and the grandmother of adult grandchildren. Occasionally when I have commented on the missing word for adult children, ageing women have said to me 'but they'll always be your babies'. Actually no, they will not. They are not. They are adults, with the privileges and responsibilities and expectations and learnings and generative capacities of adults. Maturity demands I treat them as such, with due consideration and respect for the relationship as it ferries through us through time.

What is the consequential price for a world which insists on the infantilisation of adults as children? Robert Bly's sibling society is our first clue. The connection between the infantilisation of adult children and adult grandchildren and the sweeping sentimentalisations of mothers and grandmothers of adults in our society, is our second. For it is clear to me that whilst mothers of small children have found voice in the world, at least in the west, ageing mothers of adults and grandmothers of adults are bound yet by romanticised mythologies that render them silent and bewildered by their absence of words:

> *"I had a friend I'd known for most of my life. I could say anything at all to her. I didn't see her often, but when I did we'd tell each other anything and everything – except how hurt I am by my (adult) children's behaviour. The moment I say anything at all about how I'm feeling about them my friend notices something out the window or stands up to clear the dishes or whatever. So eventually when she asked I would say, 'they're good', and leave it at that. I don't see her anymore. There is absolutely nowhere I can say I'm struggling with how hurt I am. Sometimes I want to scream 'I HATE MY FUCKIN KIDS'. And it's not that I hate them, I hate that I'm not allowed to speak about the impact of their behaviour on me. I have a top shelf in my bathroom cabinet. When the sadness gets too much I nibble a corner of Valium."*
>
> Julie

A friend recently messaged me a Facebook post, a poem about 'becoming an elder'. It was filled with mythologised sentiments about the ageing and elderly as guides for wisdom and advice. The post landed as I was reading Simone de Beauvoir, as it happens, who was furiously dismantling the rigid roles available to the ageing and elderly. The aged, wrote Simone, "are required to be an outstanding example of all the virtues", and "above all they are called upon to display serenity: the world asserts that they possess it, and this assertion allows the world to ignore their unhappiness". She continues: "The purified image of themselves that society offers the aged is that of the white-haired and venerable Sage, rich in experience, planing high above the common state of mankind; if they vary from this, then they fall below it."

Simone is not specifically speaking of women. However, in keeping with the focus of this project it is fair to say she is also speaking of women. Simone is describing Julie's experiences of the imposition by society of the narrow band of roles and expressions available to her as the mother of adults. She can speak, *but not that*. By speaking *that* she falls below 'the common state of mankind'. She may sustain quiet equilibrium. She may not express how she feels in response to the words and actions of her adult children. She may be venerable and wise. She may not be hurt and upset:

> *"My family was gathered around the table in my son's home. Both my (adult) kids were there, as well as my grandchildren. It's not often we're all in the same place. My daughter-in-law had a verbal dust-up with my son. She says to everyone around the table, naming them personally one by one, 'I'm sorry you had to experience that'. She names everyone but me, one by one she says their name. It's a funny moment. We are all laughing. I ask, 'are you sorry for me too?' And she says, 'no, you're tough'. It struck my heart like a hammer. I wanted to ask if she was sure? I was so confused that she couldn't see the hurt in me, and the unhurt in the others. It felt cruel and singled me out as separate."*
>
> Debra

## Pearling

A while back I was privy to a conversation between women that gave me a new word: *pearling*. Definition: the quiet action accompanying the shattering of a woman's heart in response to the telling of another woman's experience. The English-speaking world has a trope for this action: clutching her pearls. A clipped phrase for cruel mockery and righteous judgement of elderly women, now that I understand its meaning. Here is my introduction to pearling:

I am in the company of three ageing women. We are seated comfortably in the corner of a quiet coffee shop. Mel pulls at a loose thread on an experience about a recent holiday with her grandson. She had taken the boy rock hunting, hiking, caving. They'd camped beneath big night skies, sharing campfires with strangers, night after night watching wheeling stars through the mesh of their little tent. She'd let the boy's phone die on day one, kicking it under the car seat in the hope he'd forget his obsession with the screen.

She spoke to us of their unfurling days, the radiance in the child's eyes at week's end, his body shining with the activated, animated life-force of a beloved child; their conversation and camaraderie, the inert screen-child now engaging, alert and *interesting*. But this was not the point of her story. At week's end, she drove the child home. They were expected at dinnertime. They were hailed as heroes, the rock-hunter returned with his quarry (literally, laughed Mel). The woman's daughter-in-law had prepared a welcome feast. As the family moved towards the dinner table, Mel was in the kitchen. Her daughter-in-law slipped past her and whispered: "Make yourself something from the fridge."

*"Make yourself something from the fridge."*

Soft tears bowled along Mel's face with the telling. *Make yourself something from the fridge*. No place for her at the family table. "Make yourself something from the fridge." At those merciless words, the hands of the women in the circle flew to their chests, landing on their hearts. We were clutching our pearls. We were pearling.

And so I learned that old and ageing women are not clutching their pearls, for my generation of ageing women rarely wears them. Old and ageing women are reaching for their hearts, pierced by shattering recognition of their own experience in another woman's telling heart. This is the private language of women, made public by twisted tropes. I've watched for pearling since. You'll find it in quiet corners where women gather with friends and courage enough to share experiences that break our collective hearts.

Mel's telling of her experience prompted the women in the coffee shop to gasp the same word Debra used when she was singled out by her daughter-in-law: cruel. It is a word I have heard often inside these conversations: "how cruel", "it was cruel", "why are they so cruel?" Cruel. A strange word. Cruel … brutal, savage, vicious. Cruel is a finer word than these, a word that trips lightly off the tongue without the bitterness of its synonyms. Legal ethics scholar John Stinneford wrote that cruel spoke not to the intent of the punisher, but to the impact of the punishment. Swallowing cruel is a performative function for the ageing and elderly. That performance is demonstrative of our mastery. We swallow cruel and we show up again. And we show up again. And again. And again. And again. We walk back in the door. Useful, not included. We show up for a generation that decorates its walls with symbolic hearts and admonishes the world to 'be kind'. We swallow cruel and show up over and over and over again so they can waltz out the door leaving us with the children – useful, not included:

> *"I live in a city about two hours' drive from my son and his family. I drive up to see them all the time. Recently for one of the kids' birthdays, they came down (to the city) to see a musical. I only found out by accident they were coming. I was speechless. The theatre is down the road from where I live. I can't imagine doing that to my mother, taking a family group to see something special in her neighbourhood and not inviting her along. I was so hurt. I knew the musical was special for my grandson, so I rang*

*my son and asked if they'd drop in afterwards. My son said sure they would, and I waited and I waited and I waited and they didn't show up and they didn't call or text. I was confused. It took me three days to find the courage to ring my son. I asked how the show was. Eventually I felt brave enough to ask why they didn't come over afterwards. I think I'd been afraid of the answer. And he said, 'we forgot'. They forgot. I still don't understand. I don't understand anything at all in this story."*

Anna

"We forgot."

Cruel life-shattering nothings. Tiny arrows that bring a woman down, making real her receding place from the family heart/h.

Slow burn exile.

Sarah experienced this when her daughter's children were in their mid- and late teens. She had been a significant part of her grand-children's lives from the day they were born, involved in everything from cooking meals to hanging out washing to singing them to sleep to bicycling them to school to taking them on holidays to watching them play sport to sitting through school concerts to contributing financially, and so on. By the time the 'children' were in their mid- and late teens, a barely perceptible change in the family wind began to brush against her skin. She said it was as if her daughter was cutting her off from the herd, as if she (the daughter) were a working dog corralling sheep (the 'children'), whose mission was to cut one out (Sarah). Sarah described the pain she felt as dull at first, subtle, then sharp. It was hurtful. It was bewildering. She did not understand. She had, and has, neither words nor concept for what she was experiencing.

I don't know if you've ever skinned a sheep, but I have. It takes a thousand small cuts with a sharp blade until eventually you punch through and sever the sheep from its skin. Sarah's accounting of her experience reminded me of skinning sheep. By the time her daughter had punched through, Sarah was numb and without cognition of what had happened. She still has no concept for this outcome in her family. It caused irreparable damage to her relationships with her grandchildren and it took ten years for her to understand her daughter's message: she was, and is no longer, part of 'their' herd. And so it has proven to be, she said, as her daughter's unknown story of her became her grandchildren's story of her. Ten years of rampaging self-loathing filled the hole they left in Sarah's skin. She said, "the loss is immeasurable. I cried for years and years and years".

Sarah is describing the kind of tears that rise quickly and are just as quickly breathed away. Functional tears that belie the breaking heart of the woman at the hub of family life. The kind of tears that in private moments fill an ocean. The kind of tears only shattered women know. No longer useful, never to be included. Still we rise. Sarah kindly shared extracts from her journal writing about her experiences:

> *"Who are we when we cannot see ourselves reflected in our daughter's eyes? How is it this dreadful story, whatever it may be, took such solid root in my daughter's heart?*

> *"What did I ever do to make me so unworthy of connection, communication, any small reflection at all. What did I do? And what can I do now? The answers are clear. Nothing. Nothing except feel the emptiness as the lights go out on my daughter's orbit, and sadness floods my heart and loosens my tears. I am nothing to them. Nothing and nothing. How could my crimes have been so serious as to be worthy of this?*

> *"One of the most hurtful blows life can deal is when you think you're part of something great and you belong in that great thing. You give everything to that great thing and then you discover that you were useful, and that is all."*

The women represented in the narratives presented so far without exception speak highly of their adult children and grandchildren.

Competent, capable, well-meaning, productive, courteous, engaging people in the world. For and among others. Others, not her. Why not her? Why not her, too? Why not towards their mothers and grandmothers? Whether the disappearing of ageing mothers of adult children from the heart of western industrialised families is conscious or otherwise, it is clearly intended.

This 'disappearing' is not the voluntary action of the women themselves, although it may well eventually be, as it most certainly was for Sarah and others once they forsook all assumptions and expectations about 'belonging' in their nuclear family disasters. Rather, and firstly, ageing women *will be* disappeared by the intentional actions of others from their place at the centre of the family heart/h.

What puzzled Simone de Beauvoir is that adult children do not recognise that the slow burn exile they impose upon their mothers and grandmothers will come for them. The reality of the future that awaits them is lost on the parents of children and young adults. In the first instance they cannot imagine the children to whom they are so devoted turning on them. Secondly, they fail to understand that their own behaviour towards their mother and grandmother is teaching the children how to treat them when they are ageing and old. Slow burn exile is on their horizon and, like the rest of us, they cannot, will not, do not, refuse to see it coming until it is far, far, far too late. And they will turn to face the horrific realisation that what they inflicted on the mothers and grandmothers up the line will now be done to them. *And there is nothing they can do about it.* And here's the real gut-punch – the horror is twice-lived, through the pain of recognition of their actions up the family line, as they send apologies on the wind to a heaven they may or may not believe in, and the pain inflicted upon them down the line by the children they never imagined would turn on them. And turn they will, for we trained them well.

It is one thing to tell of the experiences of ageing mothers of adults. It is quite another to examine the impact of these experiences on her living, feeling body. After the telling of the pearling story in the café,

I contacted Mel. I was curious to know how she might language her feeling body consequent to "make yourself something from the fridge". She agreed to meet. I invited her to take up her account from the moments after her daughter-in-law's words were spoken: *make yourself something from the fridge*. Mel's experience was so painful, the memory in her body so visceral, it is worth an abridged version of her telling.

## Pearling 2: Languaging the feeling body

"I was standing at the stove, stirring leftovers from the trip. All my focus was on my eyes. It takes everything I have to hold back the tears. The tears feel threatening; if they spill over I'll wash everything away with them. My son is standing beside me making small talk, utterly oblivious to any of this. It's a struggle to keep my breath even. Then a force, it wasn't 'like' a quake it *was* a quake, this shaking force began to rumble deep in my centre, a slow rumble as if from far away. I could feel the shake begin inside me. I've never experienced anything like it. It's more than I can manage publicly. I can't stay. I look my son dead in the eye, and I say, "how is this acceptable to you?" I remember that moment. It's rock solid in my bones. I'd wanted to say that to him for so long, for years and years and years. *How is this acceptable to you!* I'm so hurt. I'm beyond hurt. My body has its own reckoning going on. I'm about to erupt. Not in anger, but in unspilled agonising pain and bewildered tears. Not eye-tears, body tears.

"The whole event is a string of moments etched into my flesh. I put down the spoon. I walked near-blind to the dining table. I kissed my older grandson firmly on the cheek. It was rough, like a pressing farewell. I did not look at his mother. I asked the darling child I'd just spent the week with to walk me to the car, gathered my things and left. The quake was erupting. A slow shake was taking hold of my body, my whole body. It was all I could do to hug the child in the dark driveway and wave him back inside. I could not see. My body shook. I was nauseous. I was not fit to drive. Three times I drove into the bushes in the curving driveway as I pulled away. I was in no condition to drive the night freeway. Yet I did. Strangely, there were no actual tears. The whole thing was internal. My body did the crying, shaking with this strange force that near-blinded me. It was choking me. I found my breath. I found more breath."

She glanced up, tears in her eyes with the telling: "That's it really, I'm not sure there's anything more I can say."

## Pearling 3: No place at the family table

Mel and I sat in the silence that comes upon mature women after such telling. Then she said, "do you know what's unbearable? As I walked to the dining table to kiss the older boy goodbye, that darling little boy I'd just spent that marvellous week with ran for a chair and dragged it to the table, creating a welcome place for me at the family table."

Mel pearls. I pearl. She begins to weep. Here is the rest of her account:

"I can still hear the chair scraping across the floor, still feel in the depths of my body the joy in his welcome to the feast. Yet I saw his action only out of the tiniest corner of my eye. That quake in my body robbed me of my senses. The force within me already had me heading for the door. I did not have capacity in the moment to stop myself and accept his welcome chair. That spontaneous, unreceived act of love will be with me for the rest of my life. *I did not receive his chair.*

"I remember sitting in the car in the darkness, knowing I was leaving my son's wife to tell the story as she liked. I know she didn't tell them about her whispered passing in the kitchen. And I know there was no place set for me at the family table. If my son had come out to speak to me in the driveway he might have paved a way for me back in the door. He did not. And I couldn't go back in.

"I was going overseas a fortnight later. I wanted some contact before I left, so I took a deep breath and went to see them. We met on the beach. I haven't been back inside that house since that incident. My young grandson was distant, waving me off as if I was stranger.

The older boy didn't look at me or speak to me when I saw him. Whatever story was woven at that family table in my absence cast me out of what small place was left to me in their lives. And now I'm just terribly terribly sad. So so sad."

## Pearling 4: The legacy

Two years later I followed up with Mel again to inquire how the experience had played out over time:

"I've never returned to that house. I've never gone back in there. The thought of it makes me nauseous and I begin to tremble. My chest pounds like I'm having some sort of heart attack. There is no safe passage for me in that house. It is my son who needs to create that for me and he acts as if nothing happened. Which to him it probably didn't. I'm haunted by the hideous memory of the little boy dragging the chair to the table, but that said, my relationship with him as we knew it ended that night. That's the other thing that makes me never ever ever want to see my son's wife again, and that is knowing that if I left the house, in some small dark corner of me I knew that if I left it was over, that his mother would blow up everything that little boy knew and trusted about his relationship with me. Inside that wonderful triumphant moment of returning home with all his rocks, shining with the opportunity to share his adventure with his parents, his spirit was shattered by a side-swipe event that was well outside his capacity for understanding the moment, and his mother would not, did not, does not have maturity enough to understand that not everything she thinks, feels, believes about other people needs to be shared with the children. It's on me too, of course, that inside the trembling and quaking and blindness I could not pull myself together and manage the situation for the sake of the child. And then I remember that it wasn't one event. It was years and years and years of rudeness and exclusion. I can't take any more."

It's worth noting that examined phenomenologically, the essence of the pearling encounter was physical. This ageing mother of adults had been cognitively rationalising her place in her son's house for years, and inside an awful situation she could rationalise it still. It was her body that could not take any more.

Slow burn exile. Useful, utterly excluded.

Sue is another ageing mother of adults who has decided her health and wellbeing depend on maintaining distance from her adult children:

> *"I've stopped proactively contacting my kids. For years, everything was a one-way conversation. I've had enough. It took about two years for my son to notice I'd gone quiet. Interestingly, and it's probably not a coincidence, this past year I've heard more from him about what he and his kids are up to than I have in years. It's all in text of course, a sentence here and there. He never uses a greeting, no hello, never says my name. I don't reply unless he asks me a direct question. After a few months of this he recently said, 'are you not engaging'. Four words! I ignored him. It's bait. He wants me to take responsibility for a conversation he wants to have. I've been here before. I used to help him through. This time I was shocked by what I wanted to say. I wanted to say: 'No son, I'm protecting myself from you'."*
>
> Sue

Sue has summoned silence as self-protection. Belinda remains bewildered by her exclusion:

> *"For three years I lived in the same city where one of my sons works. Three years and he never called in to see me, unless he was dropping off his kids for me to mind. His wife would stay in the car. She never came in. I don't understand why she did that. The only thing I can think of is when I first moved there he did call around once, for dinner. He was excited to see me. I was excited that I'd be living near my son again. The following day he called and said, 'can you tell B where I was last night?' The poor man*

*had spent all night and half the next day justifying to his wife the fact he'd had dinner with his mother. I don't know whether it was conscious or not, but he never called around again except to drop off the kids. I was at the gym one day and a man my son's age bragged to his mates about living in the same suburb as his mother and not seeing her for two years. I wanted to scratch his eyes out."*

Belinda

Slow burn exile is a blast furnace in the end.

Women who are unpartnered experience slow burn exile differently to those who are partnered. The partnered have a witness, a voice to speak on their behalf, an advocate, someone with whom to share their experience, someone to tell. Said Helen, "my husband is my champion. I don't know how I'd cope if I didn't have him to stand up for me around my son and his partner". Unpartnered ageing mothers have no witness to their relationships with adult sons and daughters and their partners. This absence of witness and confidante appears to give grave licence to the empowered sibling-raised to behave poorly towards unpartnered ageing mothers and grandmothers. Laura is the ageing mother of adults and a gratefully partnered woman. She said, "I'd be devastated without a partner. I'd be stuck. I would be in so much pain. It's too much to ask from someone to bear this kind of pain alone. I don't know what I'd do without him. I have a friend who went overseas because of the pain, and she stays away, and I understand why she does that, she had to do something because there's only her. Being (the ageing mother of adults) is a kind of displacement. Friends don't understand, and people generally have no idea what it's like".

## A change of heart

I am wandering around the neighbourhood with Laura. She tells me about her friend Meg, whose adult daughter was giving her such grief that Meg no longer has any feeling for her. Said Laura, "she's had a change of heart". We stop in our tracks to absorb the gravitas of this statement. We understood it was literal. A statement of dreadful pain, an expression of severe loss, a finality of outcome we understood Meg would never in a million years have imagined for herself. Said Laura, "she's exhausted by her relationship with her daughter. She has nothing left". The empathy Laura and I have for Meg is visceral. We can *feel* it. Our hearts beat a little faster. Our throats tighten.

Alice mirrored Meg's change of heart:

> *"My daughter is very prickly with me. I'm only allowed to speak of certain things in certain ways. I don't know what those things are, but I do know what they're not, and that's pretty much everything that matters to me. On her last visit, after a couple of days she got quite nasty and snapped at me to stop speaking rubbish. She's not usually that nasty, usually she just ignores me or yawns or looks out the window or twists my words into something they're not and then refuses to let me speak so I can clarify things. This time she was right. What I couldn't say to her, because I'm not allowed to speak, is that in my desperation to find anything at all to say to her I did speak rubbish. Whenever I see her I'm left feeling dead ashamed of myself. And now I'm out of puff. I'm done. I have nothing left for this relationship. It takes me months to get my spirits back after her visits. I'm not even sad about it. I'm past being sad."*
>
> Alice

Alice's "out of puff" reflects Meg's "change of heart" and Sue's 'protecting herself'. All are ageing mothers of adults who are done being sad. I still recall the tectonic tremor in my body when I visited my mother and felt the shock of her indifference. She had withdrawn enlivened interest from her relationships. She listened, she nodded, she said what was required, she was 'kind', she shared little to nothing of genuine meaning to herself. There is only so much a woman's heart can bear. Should you think any of these women fickle, you have scant notion of how very much a mother's heart can take.

The withdrawal of ageing mothers of adults from the hearth is a withdrawal of soul from the known world. It can be likened to what poet Patricia Monaghan identified as 'wintering'. She writes, "when winter comes to a woman's soul, she withdraws into her deepest spaces. She is more than resting. She is creating a new universe within herself, destroying what should not be revived, feeding in secret what needs to thrive". A wintered woman is the ageing woman returned with redoubled strength.

Wintering is an act of survival for ageing mothers of adults who cannot take another arrow. Wintering is living estrangement. Exile is imposed on her by others. Estrangement for the wounded ageing mother of adults is a self-imposed act of survival. Estrangement can take no more hurt, no more pain. Insiders warming their toes by the nuclear family hearth will likely say she is 'choosing' her quiet absence from the world, thus imposing upon the exiled and estranged responsibility for her own return.

Alice's 'out of puff' and Meg's 'change of heart' are emblematic of women exhausted by the effort of inserting themselves into the worlds of their adult children. Further, do not mistake Alice's 'out of puff' or Meg's 'change of heart' or even Sue's silence as a turning away from their adult offspring. They may be wintering, however like all the women represented in this book, none of us has walked away.

We have not blocked our daughters and sons. We are not 'not talking' to them. We are not refusing to have anything to do with them. We are here. Right where they left us, we are here. Any time they want to walk in our door they are welcome. Any time they want to talk to us, we are here. All they need do is call. Show an interest. Show up. And just like my mother and my grandmother and my great grandmother, the front gate will swing open when they call. Just like my mother, grandmother and great grandmother I will live in the spaces between their visits. Although in my case I have neither front gate nor front door to swing open, on the run as I am from the desolation of the family fractal front gate. I am in the world, feigning liberation from the exclusionary gaze of adult offspring and the non-gaze of adult grandchildren. The braids of our relationships exist with and without their presences, for what the sibling-young do not yet know is it is not possible to leave family. You can ignore family. You can not-talk. You can block. You can cause great relational damage. For all your exclusionary efforts you still you exist in the bloodline. Like the Hotel California, you can check out any time you like but you can never leave. You cannot break or exit the matrix of kin. The web is greater than us all.

## The omphalos of Grandmother

When my granddaughter was born the nurse thrust her into my arms so she was free to tend to the birthing needs of my seventeen-year-old daughter. I was unprepared for this moment. As I wrapped this newborn baby girl in her blanket, she opened her eyes and looked straight into mine. That moment is to this day etched into my retina and rooted like a vibrant nerve in my belly. In that moment, her grandmother was born.

The following night I held her throughout the night, wandering the hospital corridor with her in my arms. My arms were alive with what I can only describe as an imprinting, an instinctive fulfillment of my duty as her grandmother, an open channel transferring all she would need to know in this life from the ancestors of the family line, through my arms and into the body of the child. I was thirty-eight years old, and my life focus shifted to the needs of a second generation of children when I hadn't quite finished with the first.

What does it mean to be a grandmother? A grand mother.

For Lucy it means enduring "daughter abuse" lest her daughter forbids her from seeing the children. For Vicki, whose daughter-in-law refuses to allow her to see her grandchildren, it means a cosmic black hole that feels like "a neverending punch in the guts". For Helen it means "compartmentalising myself off from my grandchildren" because "I can see where it's going to lead and it's just too distressing". For countless grandmothers on the fringes of unclanned nuclear families, Deborah, for example, it means distress, disempowerment and helplessness as their grandchildren howl or grow silent as they are fed to the giant by stressed parents committed to too-busy lives.

For Diane it means giving time to the children their mothers do not give: "Our grandchildren need us. One day I was visiting and the little girl was howling about something, so I took her outside and started singing to her. The child was stunned. No one had sung to her before. What world do we live in that mothers are not singing to the children?"

Said Laura, "the slightest suggestion I make causes conflagration. Any aspirations I might have for the children are seen as criticism. Grandparents I know spend so much time thinking 'holy shit this is going to be really bad in the future'. Sometimes there's an event that will leave all the hallmarks of trauma in my body as I struggle with the anguish and powerlessness. It's nauseating, it's despairing".

In sublime summary, said Kathy: "It's not my place to have opinions."

The ancestors beg to differ. What only the ageing and elderly know is that with longevity the fracticalities in the family line come into focus. This is why the old are wise – they can see what the young and middle aged cannot, the patterns in play in the microcosm (family, clan) and the macrocosm (the world). The ageing and elderly also know there are patterns in play that are greater than one life cycle and therefore not visible, although perhaps, with wisdom, predictable. Humans are generational snowballs. As I mentioned, I've personally known six generations of women in my family. I know intimately the patterns in the family fractal up and down the line, and my eyes grow wider with wonder for this witnessing with each passing year.

A friend spoke to me of her grandmother. She told me of her father's happy childhood despite the "harshness and severity" of his mother (the grandmother). The grandmother's family was eastern

European and had fled Nazi persecution during World War II. The grandmother – a young woman at the time – bundled up three children, walked them across mountains and out of their homeland to cross a neighbouring border and from there to no-idea where. In so doing, she left behind who knows what situation for her mother, her father, her grandparents, her siblings and others to whom she was accountable and perhaps close. In so doing, she kept three children fed, clothed, safe and enspirited as they sought and found protection elsewhere. We can't all be 20th Century Fox's Maria von Trapp singing our way to freedom and celebrated stardom. Our takeaway from this anecdote is that the father's happy childhood was entirely dependent on a young woman's capacity for holding herself together despite a likely shattered heart, remade by harshness and severity that was the price and the legacy of her experience of ferrying three children to precarious safety.

The poet Christine Hollywood wrote: *There were groups of deer in big extended families, with everyone accounted for.* I do not think for a moment that second phrase is incidental. It is grandmothers who do the accounting. However, to whom do we account in our wisdom from the fringes of exile in the modern, western, industrialised nuclear family when our voices are not welcome at the hearth? Laura's voice may not be welcome in the realms of her adult children, however she says "the (grand)children need us. They benefit from having a grandparent who regularly inserts themselves in their lives. It could be anything, even just a game of fiddlesticks. There's a role for us, but it's not a generational role. That's gone. Either you live around the corner or you're non-existent".

This brings us to a nasty, misused word that has taken root in the English-speaking west. The word is 'choice'. As in 'she made her choices'. As in 'that's her choice'. As in 'her life, her choices'. There is a world of distinction between 'choice' and the alternative words we ought to be seeking: 'decision', 'options', 'action'. A *choice* is what we have when we stand in the toothpaste aisle at the supermarket *deciding* which brand of toothpaste to buy among myriad *options*. Action is reaching for the *selected* item. A choice requires two or more options to choose from and empowerment enough to select from the options available. Current usage of 'choice' is a none-too-subtle redrafting of the timeworn (gendered) trope 'she made her bed, now lie in it'. It is a careless, public shaming that absolves others from engagement and care.

We do not make choices in life we make decisions and take responsive or spontaneous actions which are often devoid of conscious decision-making. It did, after all, seem like 'a good idea at the time' and 'the right thing to do. And it is. Or was until it wasn't. These tiny steps lead us this way or that, the outcome of which can never be certain simply because there is no end to this way or that until we die. We do not choose where life will lead us, and we most certainly do not choose outcomes that come with any guarantee. In actuality we do not even choose our next step, given that our next step can only be taken into the veiled unknown from where we stand in a given moment. At best we make decisions from the options available to us, one of which is blind trust, aka action. These decisions are monumental in our mind and actioning them requires great courage. We do not choose. We decide, at best. We act from the information we have at hand, knowing that the information will be woefully inadequate for the simple reason that every decision contains the unknown and the unknown is the god part of life.

Choice in current usage is a filthy word. It loses the one who 'made her choices' in the fog of service and the melee of life. Did my grandmother make a 'choice' to spend every day and every night alone in her house a long way from everyone as an elderly woman? No she did not. There is only choice when there is an alternative, and there is only choice when at least one of the 'choices' is pleasing and other people are paying attention, thereby participating in 'her' 'choice'. There is only choice when there are financial resources enough to choose from, or increase, the available options, and even then the previous point applies. My grandmother's 'choice' would have been to have people to vacuum after, rather than vacuuming the same spotless carpet she vacuumed yesterday. Her 'choice' would have been to have her daughter and grandchildren visiting regularly and often, calling by not once a month or once a year, but meeting them through daily passage in the streets, at the shops, in her home.

My grandmother was the last of the generations raised before the normalisation of individualism's unclanned modern western family. The shock for her must have been so much greater, so much worse, than it has been for me and my generation. My grandmother protected herself by vacuuming and dusting her empty house every day. My mother agonised over her mother, driving long distances to visit her every two weeks and settling for admiring her discipline in between. Until the heralding tide came for her and, not one to vacuum or dust daily, she walked her dog and then sat with the television on while she read the newspaper. "You can have the TV or you can have me" I would say on my visits, which to my credit were regular and often. The TV or me. I failed utterly to understand that the TV was a constant friend and I was fickle as the wind. Now I am ageing, and the only one in my daily world, the people on the television are more real to me than anyone I know. Apologies on the wind to my mother in a heaven I don't believe in.

Perhaps my mother's sorrow for her lonely mother was on her ageing breath, as she spoke repetitively about her mother, and her father, grandmother and grandfather. Perhaps she was seeking redress for what she had not noticed, had failed to see, had neither acknowledged nor tended when she herself was not frail, even though she most certainly did not ignore the needs of her ailing mother. Perhaps she was hoping her adult children would hear in her stories an encoded message of her own needs (we did not). And so she remembered the old ones in holy litany when there was nothing else to do but sit in her chair and wait for the rest of us to call.

At eighty years of age, my mother went to the top of the public housing list. She elected to live in one of Australia's favourite beachside holiday towns, reasoning her adult children and grandchildren would visit her there. I used to think that was a smart move, and funny. That it was true I now recognise as heartbreaking. My mother knew she was not enough for any of us to go out of our way to see her for no other reason than we wanted to see her, not in any real or regular way, and even then the beach town drew most of her family to her gate on occasional visits at most. They were, after all, 'busy' and 'had their own lives to lead'.

Ageing women who live alone know they've crossed the line between pre-ageing and ageing with a single momentary realisation: 'I can die in the night and no-one will know':

> *"I was visiting my son and his family and they asked how*
> *I'd been. I told them I'd been sicker than I've ever been in my life*
> *with the flu, that I couldn't get out of bed, barely ate for a week*
> *My daughter-in-law said, 'why didn't you tell us?' and*
> *I thought 'you'd know if you ever called'."*
> Jennifer

Jennifer's debilitating flu brought into focus the shock she could be dead for "days, weeks or months" and no-one would notice. I think of my grandmother in her empty house and wonder if it was being unnoticeably dead that played on her mind or the matter of tending to her body.

In my grandmother's time there were rituals the sibling-raised in the modern west were required to undertake to lay out her bones (we did not). Being unnoticeably dead is one thing. What of the daily desolation of knowing no-one would notice should she fail to rise? That she would not be missed – which is not a fair statement to make on behalf of my mother and her brothers, but the point stands, her absence from the world would be unnoticed until they noticed, and her dying would be unwitnessed. In my grandmother's world, no-one was watching her or watching out for her in any real way, although no doubt some of them thought they were and others actually were by the standards of our time. Certainly not by the standards of her own time.

It is an extraordinary cruelty in the west that at the same moment the ageing and elderly become physically vulnerable, there is no-one on hand to help. Said Kathy, "yes it does hurt at times, but my daughters are really clear – they don't want to have to look after me. It's scary, because who the fuck is going to if not them?" She added, "if my father hadn't died and left me some money I'd be completely fucked". And then, "but what else can I expect when I look at how I treated my mother. Because, you know, I didn't teach them to look after me".

A similar realisation dawned on Leanne during our interview, as she explained her reasoning for not allowing her mother to see her children when they were young. Heartbreakingly for Leanne, a generation later her daughters do not allow her to see their children. Their reasoning? Word for word an echo of Leanne's reasoning for exiling her own mother. That Leanne's daughter will hear the same words from her own daughters is a matter of time. The family fractal, repeating at scale.

When my grandmother vacuumed her spotless house she did so without complaint on knobbled feet and a waddling body stiff from a lifetime of work. What I failed to notice until mine was the ageing body is how painful that must have been for her. When my mother woke each morning she would talk me through the wonder of her waking exercise routine before she got out of bed (over and over and over again). What she really wanted me to hear was, 'I hurt'. Ageing hurts. People would say about both these women, 'she's remarkable for her age'. Now I say, because I have two words my mother and grandmother did not: 'fuck off'. That the physical pain of ageing was amplified and exacerbated by the physical pain of their breaking hearts makes a beggar out of belief. And so I have two more words, for us all: 'pay attention'. Living with a broken heart is agony. Lucy was so overwhelmed when her daughter turned on her she suffered panic attacks:

*"I was consumed by anxiety. I was always nauseous. I would do anything to make her stop judging me. I jumped through all her hoops trying to solve whatever her problem was. One day I realised she was bullying me, like domestic violence. These days I make an effort to say 'no'. Sometimes I fail, but it's a fine line because I have to keep her on side so I can see my granddaughters."*

Lucy

When Leanne's daughters ceased communication with her she said the pain was so unbearable she considered suicide:

*"When our relationships first broke down it was that devastating I could feel it all over my body. It was horrendous. I considered suiciding, as I took it all on board myself. The guilt – what did I do, what didn't I do? I gave so much of myself away to them. Now I've drawn a line and it immediately felt good, all the pain left my body. It was absolutely the right thing, but knowing it was 'the right thing' and feeling proud of myself for doing that is devastating, but I knew if I backed down and let them treat me like shit to keep those relationships, that was not good."*

Leanne

By drawing her line in the sand, Leanne took action to save her own life. Jennifer too acted to save her own life when her adult children's relentless disrespect and carelessness left her with a singular thought: "It's me or them." Unable to bear the left-behindness of her life, Jennifer has fled her home:

*"I spent ten years feeling that much shame about all the things that were wrong with me I wanted to die. I couldn't bear the pain. In the end I sold up and went overseas. My son and his wife have the loneliest children I have ever met. It breaks my heart. One day I realised I've done all I can do for them. I can't save them from their parents. The thought of going back to Australia makes me feel sick to my stomach. I'm absolutely fine when I never hear*

*from them. When I do, and fortunately that's not often, I could*
*weep forever for what has been lost, for me and the children."*
Jennifer

For decades now, fuelled by the increasing influence of the mental health and new age industries, populist narrative has ratcheted up the blame on 'mother' for what 'she did' to cause her daughters' and sons' progressively deepening 'issues', perhaps better described as social contagions. People say adolescent girls are mean. They're nothing compared to what's lying in wait for the ageing mother of adults. What remains unrecognised is that adult offspring create their mothers, just as surely as the converse is true. Years of shaming, blaming and slow burn exile cannot but impact on the personality, behaviour, relationships, health and wellbeing of the ageing mother in the world, thereby creating, then reinforcing, then 'proving' the story of 'mother'. *We know what mothers are like.* Even if she is the monster you say she is, where is this love and kindness you insist upon in the world? Love and kindness that is performative is neither loving nor kind. I have spoken to ageing mothers of adult children who acted to save themselves. Where's the study that asks the question from those who tipped themselves off the back of the canoe?

For those of us who are mothers, there are one or two, or perhaps a few more, people in the world who will ever call us by that sacred name: 'Mum.' Sarah didn't know this until the word grew silent on the wind:

*"I don't know if you've noticed, but people these days don't say*
*hello when they text. I only hear from my kids when they text,*
*so I rarely hear their voices. I'll get three words from my son —*
*'how you doing?' I don't answer any more. What am I supposed*
*to say to that? He's asking me to take the time to type a message*
*on the phone when he can't be bothered sharing anything at*
*all with me. He doesn't address me, he doesn't tell me anything*
*about his life and he doesn't reply if I do take time to answer*

*him – and I don't call a 'like' emoji or 'heart' emoji a reply.*
*My daughter's the same. Just before Christmas last year I got*
*a text from her saying 'what are you doing for Christmas?'*
*I was excited. I thought she was going to invite me somewhere.*
*It turned out she had a friend who needed a cat sitter."*

Sarah

Sarah wound up spending Christmas Eve wandering the aisles of her local mall, humming along to Christmas carols in the company of last-minute shoppers.

For me, the world's most wondrous word, accounting for language and synonym, is 'Nanny'. When my grandchildren were children I saw them nearly every day. Whenever I called by, they would run to the door calling "Nanny!" When they were in early high school a shadow moved into their home. The shadow parked them on big chairs in front of a big screen and initiated them into television streaming. I can still feel the awful thwack in my chest the day I walked in the door and neither they nor the shadow glanced up from the television. The children had been fed to the giant. Half their lifetime later the world has fallen silent. The last time I heard my granddaughter speak my name was in a dream. I heard her voice in the night: "Nanny." It was a reaching, a plea. I hired a private investigator to assure me she was well-enough and not lost to life's vile underbelly.

I can still hear the last time any of my four grandchildren said "Nanny". It was on a busy city street, when the youngest, in his middle primary school years, a child who had loved me with all his heart and has now been fed to the giant, was walking away with his parents. He glanced back and in a small voice said to no-one in particular, "Nanny". When no-one speaks our name, we cease to exist. I think of the children now as lifely ghosts. They are my past. They are not my present. I don't know about my future. My funeral doesn't count.

Tiny arrows that bring a woman down.

Leanne knows what I mean. She lives in a small town and is not allowed to speak to her grandchildren, who live a block away from her house:

> *"They would keep coming round and I'd have to say 'you're not allowed to be here' and send them home. And now when I come across them in town we're all confused. They look at me. They know I've seen them. And then I turn away because I can't cope. I think I'm doing the right thing, that I'm saving them from the situation, and then I think 'what if they think I don't want to see them'. It's heartbreaking, absolutely heartbreaking."*
>
> Leanne

Like Jennifer, Leanne has now left her home rather than bear the agony of staying in the same town as her grandchildren. Whereas Jennifer sold up and moved overseas, Leanne housesits for others. In doing so, both ageing women have forsaken their places of belonging in their community and in society. They are women untethered from time and place.

Lucy and Leanne are friends who reconnected after many years. Up until a twenty-minute phone call one despairing day, Lucy had believed she was a "monster".

> *"I was that ashamed of myself. I thought I was a monster. All my friends had fantastic relationships with their kids, they're all happy families, and I was the worst. It's only with Leanne that I've been able to say how painful it is."*
>
> Lucy

Lucy has a Facebook feed that belies her relationship with her daughter. Her public face is one of happy families. I asked her about the possibility her friends may also be faking it, that like her they may be feeling isolated and silenced by shame. Lucy is stunned. It never occurred to her that others might also be masking their family existence. I asked her why she presents a polished public face when the reality is so different. She said, "so I can experience the life I should be living".

Laura also does not speak to her friends about her experiences with her adult children: "People can only hear gossip or schadenfreude. There's this happy families thing where it's not okay to have conflict, so you really can't share it. One awful January I did share it with a friend and she said, 'oh I know what the problem is – it's you'. These days I go easy on myself. I take a gummy (medical marijuana) when I'm going over to see the kids, so I won't be seen as the problem."

Recently in one of my writing groups, two small remarkable events occurred. One participant wrote a poem about her lack of worth, and I misread the second line. Where in reference to her children she had penned 'what a gift I have been given', I read 'what a gift am I'. I mentioned this in the group. Another woman had also misread those tender words: what a gift am I. *What a gift am I.* Later on in the same session, a participant spoke of the writing miracle she had experienced during the week:

> *"I've been struggling to write about my mother, because I don't want to seem disloyal, but I want to speak the truth – she was awful. And then I started writing and I remembered how wonderful she had been. The pen remembered for me."*
>
> Jane

The pen remembered for me. The pen is also remembering for my friend Alison. We are sitting on her verandah sipping a good Argentine red while the sun goes down. Alison is telling me about the book she wants to write about her mother. She is making amends: "I was so critical of her! She did nothing wrong yet I judged her for years. I was appalling. I acted like she was the worse mother in the world. She wasn't terrible at all!" Jane and Alison have found in the reverent privacy of writing, maturity and friendship what they have been denied in therapy, contemporary western society and television – genuine love, respect, admiration and even reverence for their mother.

Community feeling eclipses private logic. Wouldn't it be something if we could find this place while they are living? I know now, for example, why my mother stopped listening to music or watching movies. It was to protect her heart from cycling memories and visceral hurt that pierced her body without warning. And why she turned on her radio when she woke in the deep end of night. It was to drown out the noisy ghosts in her head shouting vicious judgement about crimes she could not perceive. The radio was her surrender to the endless compulsion to rise again and again when our tiny arrows brought her down. In the wake of her surrender to rising no more came the noisy ghosts of bewildering judgement: *but what did I do?* Perhaps endless sadness is a potion for cultivating genuine capacity for compassion and kindness.

When my mother offered to do things for me and I pushed back, I failed to comprehend that she was offering me the last of what she had to offer. She was not 'telling me what to do'. She was offering me guidance. She was not encroaching on me and my precious independence, and she was not intruding on my life. I was her life.

The tides of the mothers are written in tears. I know many among the empowered middle aged who claim they have been silenced as they broadcast each moment's 'mytruths' to the world, what author Jeanette Winterson might describe as "the daily stupidity of our childish feelings". If you have words and an amphitheatre in which to proclaim them to people who are cheering you on, you are not experiencing the state of being silenced. Being silenced is to be without words. Being silenced is to enter the courageous state of overcoming to find your words. Being silenced is to choke on your words knowing even if you do find them and can get them past your throat you know there's not a soul on earth who is interested in hearing what you have to say and that a million others are lined up to deny your experience if it does not align with their mythology of the ageing mother and grandmother of adults.

Oh how lucky we are to have them.

The realisation that my grandmother may possibly have felt about the birth of her eldest granddaughter (me) the way I still feel about the arrival of my granddaughter is a bone-chilling sorrow, for her loss and my failure. That this most primal of relationships is denied fruition on its own terms in the modern western society is a catastrophe. The dissembled mythologising of mother and grandmother in social narrative and television, such as the two are still distinguishable, is ruinous for individuals and family relationships, and by extension to community, world and planet. To those who tell us we are so lucky to have them I say, they are lucky to have us. The truly favoured get to keep us.

# 4.

## The Cost of Living

THE COST OF living is an economic measure. It is, literally, the financial resources an individual adult or family (nuclear of course) needs to pay for 'basic resources'. Such resources are considered to be housing, food and fuel. Healthcare is often factored in; inclusions such as entertainment and public transport are dependent on the focus of the economic analysis. Always, the cost of living pertains to humans as units and is measured in numbers preceded with a dollar sign.

This way of measuring is emblematic of the age of corporate individualism, where an individual's worth is measured by their capacity to generate income and contribute to 'the economy'. The ageing and elderly, therefore, like the children, are inherently burdensome, given they cost more than they contribute. The children are forgiven their dependency in the modern west, consigned to spending (economy word) inordinate amounts of time in daycare so their parents might earn enough money to provide a home, pay other people to mind them and feed them when they get home. Or so their parents can build a career and 'have it all'. The ageing and elderly are a problem. They take more than they give, and the thought bubbles with a marketing plan have coined a new term for adult offspring with children of their own – they are the 'sandwich generation' and 'their issues' (pop psychology word) are firmly girded by the adults who birthed them and the children they birthed. The sandwich generation woman finds herself 'overburdened' (sandwich word) by the 'care needs' (policy words) of others and 'pressured' (sandwich word) to find time to 'achieve her personal goals' (marketing phrase), as if the problem is those needing care rather than familial and industrial systems that do not serve anyone but the already wealthy and those who are willing to forsake everything to dine at their table. The ageing and elderly, like the children, need what sibling adults in modern western societies claim not to have: time, attention, money, care. Such burdensomeness is mitigated by the degree to which the ageing and elderly are 'useful', for example, the provision (economy word) of 'childcare' (policy word).

For the ageing and elderly, the cost of living is an expansive concern. Housing, food and healthcare are the knife edge between living and dying. Entertainment, fuel and public transport determine their capacity to participate in the world. These too are life and death concerns, given the cost of loneliness and isolation are as impactful on human health and the national health budget as, say, obesity and smoking.

For the unclanned ageing mother and grandmother, her capacity for meeting the cost of her living depends upon her economic circumstances at the moment her income earning capabilities run dry. Is she partnered, unpartnered, untethered? Has she inherited money or has she no inheritance? Does she benefit from the economic resources of a partner through death, divorce or shared living costs? Does she have lifelong savings or a superannuation plan? The reality that her earning capacity is time limited can sideswipe an ageing woman, considering her working capabilities peak at the juncture of fading visibility. It was a shock to my mother to find her value to the work world was time-limited, despite her passion for and capacity to continue working reliably and effectively. It was a shock to my grandmother to find her value to the world was time-limited, despite her tremendous organisational skills and capabilities. And even though I witnessed their confusion and loss it didn't occur to me that my earning capacity – and therefore my value in the world – would be time-limited too.

Naturally, I had seen my mother's and grandmother's loss as sad problems for them. They were individual concerns rather than systemic spites the ageing face with the dawning realisation that regardless of their skill level, they are no longer employable and are therefore, by definition, of no value (economy word). This is more than an academic observation of interest to social justice warriors and policy-makers. It heralds the rapid advance of a gargantuan tide – swathes of ageing and elderly people living without purpose and, unless they have foundational wealth, without self-generated income. My mother, grandmother and I are not alone in the world of women who exhausted their financial reserves juggling their own needs with the needs of their children and grandchildren. That we did so willingly and with love does not change the cold reckoning *there is no more money coming*. Our lives are not lived as individuals, yet the measure of our contribution and worth is assessed as such.

Claire is an ageing woman who lives in a house she inherited from her mother. The house was also left to Claire's daughters, who, Claire presumed, would inherit when she died. Not so. Claire's house is on the market. Her daughters want the money. Their pressure is more than Claire can bear. She is hoping there will be enough money to buy a small unit when the debt is settled. Please don't say 'that was her choice'. Instead, let us ask, what is the true cost of living for the unclanned, unpartnered ageing and elderly mother and grandmother in the individualised modern west? It is more than economic. It is social, domestic, relational, political, systemic, temporal, geographic and existential. *They want us dead.* Which may in fact be a reasonable ask, given the increasing longevity of first world humans and the concurrent grip the contemporary monsters have on the sibling psyche. *We are supposed to be dead.* So they can have the house.

Jackie is a New Zealander whose adult son lives in Australia. Her son, who has a primary school-aged boy, had recently separated from his wife. Jackie knew the boy was struggling and rang her son to suggest he fly the boy over for a holiday, to give the child a break from the situation at home. Her son agreed, but said the timing was financially challenging while he and his wife sorted out their finances. That makes sense, thought Jackie, and decided it was worth whatever it cost to set the boy's spirits right. She told her son if he flew the boy over with a financial contribution she would cover the rest. A fortnight later Jackie was startled to see photos of her son and his wife on a European holiday together. She had no idea they were going overseas. A few weeks after that the entire family (nuclear) went to Africa for a month. During the boy's visit, Jackie learned the child had flown business class on points. Her son's contribution was $500. Jackie's savings were gone. What do we make of this story? Please don't say 'that was her choice'.

It costs money to grandmother (verb) in the modern west:

> *"I used to take my eldest grandson out for expensive dinners I really couldn't afford. Then I started to wonder why I was paying for his meal when he had more money than me and we only ever talked about him. He had no interest in me. I realised I was terrified I'd never see him if I didn't offer him something he couldn't resist. Eventually I stopped inviting him for dinner and I haven't heard from him since."*
>
> Allie

Claire, Jackie and Allie's experiences are mirrored in some form by all the ageing mothers of adults interviewed for this project. The price Allie paid for her decision to no longer buy expensive meals for her grandson correlates to why Claire is selling her house. Claire, who has grandchildren, is unwilling to find to out what happens if she doesn't bow to her daughters. The empowered middle aged are a force, and they are righteous in their exertion of that force. For the unclanned ageing and elderly mother and grandmother, particularly the unwealthy and/or unpartnered and untethered, those who are without witness, confidante or champion, the stress and distress of facing this force alone is overwhelming. When Kathy said, "it's not my place to have opinions", she also said, "when I say the wrong thing it turns me to stone". After that she said, "things might be different for women who have purchasing power within their families". She means grandmothers with money.

Purchasing power. Women with money have more than an economic advantage. They have an emotional and inclusionary advantage. Purchasing power is the capacity to use the former to buy the latter. Laura is a wealthy woman whose husband is in need of a great deal of care. She was referencing purchasing power when she said, "the kids have to give back", by which she means her adult children must help her with their father. She added, "although I'm not sure about the correlation between their willingness to help and shoring up their inheritance". Purchasing power. It costs money to offer children ice-creams, take them on holidays, buy them birthday gifts and 'mind' the children, all of which can cripple an unclanned, unpartnered ageing woman's capacity to participate in family life:

> *"A while back I minded my grandkids for two months while their parents went overseas. My son and his wife left me with $300 a week for food and all their needs. I discovered the day they were returning to school the youngest boy had a huge hole in the bottom of his shoe, so he needed new shoes. Then there were birthday party invitations and that meant buying presents. The cost of having children who are used to having everything is exorbitant and I was in a constant battle. It cost me a fortune to mind those kids at a time when I wasn't earning any money because I was minding the kids. I told my son how distressing it had been not having enough money to get by and my daughter-in-law said, 'do you want more money?' And I thought 'why are you asking me that?' She was making their neglect my responsibility when the right thing to do was reimburse the money. The day after they got home, I went shopping with my daughter-in-law for the weekly groceries. She spent $500 on all the things the*

> *children might like. They expected me to do everything for the*
> *kids on $300 a week and she spends $500 just on food."*
>
> Sally

Such is the cost of Sally's living. Please don't say her availability to be with the children was 'her choice'. However, she has drawn a line:

> *"I'm tired of showing up just for the privilege of having them*
> *in my life. It's all give and nothing comes back. Other women*
> *I know take what they get, but I'm done with it. It's draining*
> *the life out of me. I'm never spending money on them again,*
> *not so much as an ice-cream for kids who have more money in*
> *their bank accounts than I earn in a fortnight. If my son wants*
> *his children minded they can give me the money they need*
> *to keep them in the manner they're accustomed."*
>
> Sally

Sally did not draw a line because her son did not leave her with enough money to mind the children while he and his wife were overseas. Rather, she understood "too late" that her perpetual availability had impacted on her earning capacity during the last of her income-earning years. Like my mother, and like me, Sally had not foreseen the gateway of financial opportunity closing before she herself was ready to close it.

For the unclanned, unpartnered, untethered, not-wealthy ageing mother, birthdays and Christmases can be exponentially more expensive for her than for her wealthier adult offspring. Why? Because, in Sally's case for example, she buys a gift for each individual in her son's family, while they buy just one for her 'from everyone'. This is also the case for Allie, or would be if her son and daughter-in-law bought her gifts. They do not. Allie is in tears as she speaks:

> *"Every year I buy them all presents, birthdays and Christmas.*
> *I can't believe I'm even saying this, I'm so ashamed to say it, but*
> *I never get a present from them. At first I took it in my stride.*

*Then one time my daughter-in-law was telling me all about the Tiffany's necklace she had bought her mother for her birthday. I wondered why she was telling me this when I had received nothing. Another time we all went to my sister's place for Christmas and my daughter-in-law took a beautiful gift for my sister, but she had nothing for me. I presumed my daughter-in-law wasn't raised with a tradition of gift-giving, but the one time I was invited to her parents' house for Christmas there were presents galore, even for me, but not from my son, my daughter-in-law or from either of their children. One day I was driving along with her and I burst into tears, and asked why I never received a gift and she said 'but what would I buy you?' I was scrambling to answer this and muttered something about a candle, so for the last couple of years I've received a candle for Christmas. It's insanely awful. But that's not the worst of it – I have never received a single gift from either of my grandchildren. There's not a single treasure or keepsake I have that they made or bought for me."*

Allie

Other ageing mothers interviewed for this project also endure the pain of adult children ignoring birthdays, Christmas Day, Mother's Day. Christmas Day can be a particularly challenging time for ageing mothers of adults at the omphalos stone of estrangement. Said Maree, "my mother used to say hope springs eternal in women. She loved Christmas so much, and it breaks my heart to think every year she might have been hopeful we'd all turn up at Christmas. Every year, we all pleased ourselves about what we'd do for Christmas Day, whether we'd show up or not show up and of course not showing up meant we were doing something that didn't include her. And now I am the one who loves Christmas so much and isn't invited to whatever they're doing. It's easy not to care about Christmas when one has family who do. When one has family who don't, or at least don't care about you at Christmas, it's an awful time of year".

Allie laughed with astonishment when she spoke of her most recent family Christmas:

> *"It wasn't till about halfway through Christmas Day I realised*
> *I hadn't bought a single gift for either of my children or any of*
> *my grandchildren. I hadn't given it a thought. I was shocked!*
> *Partly because I'd forgotten them, but also because I felt nothing*
> *about it. I love Christmas. I love buying gifts and wrapping*
> *them up. After years and years of being ignored at Christmas*
> *and giving gifts and receiving nothing from my son and*
> *his family, I'm free. This year it's as if none of them existed*
> *on Christmas Day and that was such a relief."*
> Allie

Jennifer said she had exhausted herself trying to explain to her adult offspring the importance of teaching their children the value of gift giving:

> *"Surely they can give the kids $5 and teach them the pleasure of*
> *wandering around a market thinking about what they'd like to*
> *buy someone other than themselves. It was something my mother*
> *taught us to do and I taught my kids to do. They loved finding*
> *presents and handing over the money. It was empowering.*
> *So I don't understand why their little ones never get to*
> *experience the pleasure of shopping for someone other*
> *than themselves, or making something for others."*
> Jennifer

What Jennifer understands and her adult children do not is that the process of gift-giving is an honouring, not only of the individual but *the relationship*. Scholar Lewis Hyde, in addressing the reciprocal nature of gifts, observed that gifts in this sense are not transactions but an essential ritual for strengthening ties. Gifts are salutations, they are acknowledgements in motion, they are a dynamic exchange of lifeforce that reinforces bonds and renews relationships. Gifting is a cycle that fortifies and makes visible that which is in danger of being lost through lack of nurturing – the relationship itself. Jennifer, you will recall, has moved overseas rather than face the ongoing pain of engagement with her adult children:

> *"One year I gave my fifteen-year-old grandson a guitar for his*
> *birthday. He has a gaming addiction and rarely leaves his*
> *room, so I thought a guitar might be something else he could do*
> *in there. He grunted and didn't even take off the wrapping. It sat*
> *in the corner of his bedroom for a year unopened. His parents*
> *have never expected him to thank people, so it was too*
> *much to expect thanks. But I did expect his parents*
> *to open it and encourage him to play."*
> Jennifer

I am sitting with a group of five intelligent, competent, vibrant, engaging women who have come together specifically for the purpose of discussing their experiences of being the ageing mothers of adult children. When Caroline speaks, it is as if a sacred veil enwraps the group. I have not edited Caroline's outpouring:

> "The ugly truth is we are not the creatives and artists and writers we are and should be because the whole fucking shitzone of bloody family and full responsibility, you know, the almost exclusive burden of caring and nurturing and reassuring and, and, you know, sinking into the background and sacrificing. I was talking to a friend the other day and she muttered 'oh god, I'm tired. I'm so tired of giving'. And and you know I, that's the, that's the way I feel, you know. But the the hoi polloi, you know, the mainstream opinion, I don't know if they're really ready to be listening, you know, to what a cage, what a prison, what a, you know, the death of self identity, the whole question of family relationships is for women. The current generation has all these mental health conditions or difficulties or cognitive

complexes or some sort of historical trauma and all this manufactured pain, you know, and no matter how formidable I am, you know, no matter what my reservoirs are, I can't help my daughter. No, I can't. No. You know it's so fucking, you know, can I please die now. I can't bear, you know, another odyssey like this, where it's so … I'm managing this black hole of emotion in me and I just want to tear my eyes out. And you know, I've, I've given her my life, so there is, there is an aura of complete incredulity, you know what I mean, she took everything from me and yet she is the walking wounded, in every aspect of her life, and it gets to the point where death would be a relief."

It gets to the point where death would be a relief. There are four other women in this conversation. Each one of them nods in recognition. They too know what it is to experience vast and prolonged periods of darkness, hellholes of isolation and loss of place in the family. Death would be relief from the endless silent withheld-from-the-world pain of being the ageing mother of adults. To the outside world they are strong, funny women who appear to be embedded in family lives. They are 'so lucky to have them'. Yet all have been through or are inside tunnels of pain so dark they secretly long to tip themselves off the back of the canoe. And yet they rise. They show up. They smile. It might take a gummy but they keep going. Despite the absence of return on their gifts and their giving, they keep going. Despite the price they pay for that absence, they keep showing up.

Lewis Hyde warns that failure to participate in gift exchange, the vital cycle of renewal and return, has dire consequences. In a word, "depletion". When gifts become commodities, he says, they lose their regenerative qualities. When grandmother's care becomes 'childcare', it assumes a measurable value to the economy. It is commodified. Useful, not included. When her giving is unsupported, even neglected, as in Sally's case when her son left her with insufficient funds to care for the children while he and his wife enjoyed an extended luxury holiday, Sally's gift to her son's family was commodified. Useful, neither included nor respected.

Caroline summed up depletion's ultimate consequences for ageing mothers of adults for whom the pain can become so great, when she said, "death would be a relief". The stress and distress of the commodification of the ageing mother and grandmother is a mortal reckoning. There is public discussion aplenty about baby boomers supporting their adult children. I hear zilch about well-off adult children supporting ageing and elderly mothers and grandmothers. What is the price she pays for participation in her/your family? When she spends $5 on a colouring-in book for a great grandchild, only to see the child toss it without interest with no interjection from the child's parents, please understand that the price of that book was her coffee that day, and the price she paid was more than coffee – the coffee she sacrificed for the child's gift was her social interaction, her only social interaction that day.

What are the consequences of such an encounter on the enspirited body of an eighty-five-year-old woman who lives alone? She is an elderly woman responsible for supporting herself while all around her, her adult sons and daughters and grandsons and granddaughters live the lives of Riley. She buys the children small gifts. She receives no gifts in return. She counts herself lucky when she receives a phone call. She keeps her head high. She is renowned for her 'wisdom', which is one of two personalities Simone de Beauvoir tells us is available to the ageing and elderly. She is so wise. Depleted, but wise. Longing now and then to tip herself off the back of the canoe, but wise. Sad, but wise. Lonely, but wise. Invisible, but wise. Irrelevant, but wise. She's so lucky to have them. And she would agree with you. At least on the face of it.

This wise-ness is an act of survival, battle shield for lonely, measure of the cost of her living. My mother became kinder as she grew older. It was all that was left to her when the only people she saw reliably and regularly were shopkeepers, when her newspaper and coffee were carefully budgeted for and her daily trip to town for the paper over coffee was the social highlight of her life. Either that or stay home. Alone. And measure the cost of her living against that.

If the cost of living for ageing mothers of adults were to be accounted for in the national health budget, it would be measured through the impact on her spirits and her body of the withdrawal of all expectation of interest, care, support and engagement from those she loved and loves still, and, of course, it would be measured in the overbearing pressure of the burdensome state of longing to die. And yet in a society that prioritises the accumulation of money above all else, thereby mistaking money for wealth, symbol for substance, the prolonged agonies and sadnesses of ageing and elderly mothers of adults, and the children for that matter, is of individual concern. It is a 'your' problem.

This is reflected in the none-too-subtle sibling trope, often the final stand of ageing mothers in withdrawal: 'she has to make her own mistakes'. Does she? Does she really? The impact of this familiar refrain is writ large on the bodies and spirits of young women and children bereft of guidance from ageing mothers and grandmothers. When ageing mothers withhold their experiences, knowledge and guidance, or the sibling adults they raised refuse to heed them, humanity is destined to repeat forevermore the same 'mistakes'. Young women and children, particularly girls, cannot be protected from rakes and sexual predators if 'she has to make her own mistakes'.

This trope is not wise counsel. It is a disavowal of obligation by the ageing and elderly who no longer speak, lest they upset the sibling adults they raised. It is also an abrogation of responsibility by the sibling middle aged, who deny influence to the ageing and elderly mothers in the nuclear family. The ensuing and highly measurable consequences for the national budget of rakes and sexual predators cuts across a range of portfolios and can be measured in *billions*. Such are the reverberations of the refusal to invite the thirteenth fairy to the princess's party. It spans generations and the cost of living is paid by the spirits and bodies of young women and children without guidance. It is paid in currency by the national budget and in kind by individuals.

## The omphalos of estrangement

For all of human time, right up until the later middle part of the twentieth century, almost all healthcare, medicine, healing and daily care was undertaken by mothers and grandmothers. This placed mothers and grandmothers at the epicentre of family and community life, in direct relational engagement with the people of her world, for the entirety of her life. Millennia of hands-on healing wisdom has been reduced by the infant western mind to 'folk medicine' and outsourced to technology and prodigious profit. The health and healing responsibilities of mothers and grandmothers, and consequent family and community entanglements, involved three vital attributes of human engagement: knowledge, touch, respect. At the omphalos stone of living exile in modern western nuclear families, ageing and elderly mothers and grandmothers are bereft of this gift exchange. It is fair to say, based on research, government policies and ageing mothers' experiences of life at the coalface of marginalisation, few people are interested in what she knows. Depending on her purchasing power, she is likely to be reliant on paid massage or small grandchildren for human touch. She is living a calamitous failure of respect. Consequently, ageing mothers of adults pick their way through what Caroline calls "the remainder table".

My mother sewed, knitted, cooked, cleaned, worked full-time, did what she could to protect herself and her children from their angry father/her husband and gave us adventures and Christmases she could not afford. I may not have got everything I wanted (a horse) but I ask you, what more did I want from her? Fast forward and I did all this (minus the husband) for two now adult children and helped out with most of it for two now adult grandchildren (again with no contributing father). I ask you, what more did they want from me? My mother spun gold from straw. As did I. As did my grandmother.

As did my adult daughter. As have mothers and grandmothers the world over throughout time. What more do we want from them?

Here's what's more – we expect them, the ageing and elderly, to fend for themselves, spinning gold from straw left behind on the remainder table. We require eighty-year-old mothers and grandmothers to 'take responsibility' for their own survival. Individualists in the modern westernised nuclear family, and economy, find no disjuncture between her survival and the overwhelm of material assets and resources they have stockpiled on the back of her spinning capacities. Her failure to 'save' for her retirement was, after all, 'her choice'. Many ageing women in the modern west do of course have retirement incomes. If they didn't acquire money through inheritance or divorce (commonly generated from the superior salaries and inheritances of men), they did so throughout their working lives via, in Australia for example, government-mandated superannuation schemes. None of which accounts for the disrupted work prospects of mothers and/or the catastrophes that can strike a human life and topple financial wellbeing, self-inflicted or otherwise. Ageing and elderly mothers navigate all this in the world on their own, and, in return, the western industrialised nuclear family finds fault with 'mother'.

There are times in a woman's life when a dollar is an exorbitant sum of money and an hour an impossible amount of time. In conjunction, these too are the measure of the cost of her living. Maree is at the omphalos stone of estrangement from her adult children. She speaks of getting herself back on her feet during a financially challenging time:

> *"One evening I joined them for dinner. I chose the venue because I knew they had $2 sushi, although even that was beyond my budget. The alternative was to stay home on my own in the dark. I watched as the others ordered their meals while I ordered the white plate on the sushi train. Dishes of tempura prawns, eggplant, tofu agedashi arrived at our table with my cucumber sushi. I felt the*

*vulnerability of being on the edge of society, dangerously close to being unable to participate. On the way home, I decided to drive up the highway instead of the back road. There's a rest stop on the highway for travelers and I wanted to see how many people had pulled in there for the night. I pictured my mattress in the back seat and wondered if it would come to this ..."*

Maree

Cucumber sushi was, after all, Maree's 'choice', just as whether or not to sleep in the car would be 'her choice'.

In the modern western industrialised family, and economy, the primary job of the ageing and elderly is to not be a burden to their family or society. After decades of devotion, regardless of the familial, social, economic, political, industrial conditions of her living, that is her remaining task: not to be a burden. Among the dastardly messages peddled by ad men and marketeers are the pre-paid funerals that make explicit this until relatively recently implicit dictate. It is as insane as billing the children for childcare. Surely the least the living can do is bury us.

As well as financial wellbeing, the cost of living for ageing mothers and grandmothers can and ought to be measured in *relational* terms, that is measuring the actualities of her living as an assemblage of place and people in her world. For example, isolation, exile, the absence of touch, bewilderment, grief, ongoing physical pain and a haunted longing to die are all exacerbated or mitigated by her partnered, unpartnered or untethered status in the world. Said Helen, "I don't know how I'd cope without my husband. The family situation would rip me to bits. With my husband at least they (her adult children) are accountable to someone. I have a companion to share it with, a champion, someone to call them to account".

Where Helen has a champion to mitigate her bewilderment and grief about isolation and exile from the family hearth, infusing her world with touch and assuaging the longing to die rather than live with the pain of exclusion, the unpartnered, such as Kathy and Lucy, are isolated and alone. The untethered, such as Jennifer and Leanne, are without anchor in the world. Said Kathy, "as soon as my daughters got married things changed. They turned their attentions to their husbands. I was abandoned. Now they're so involved in the role of parenting they're always critiquing me at the same time. How does it make me feel? I guess I shut down. I withdraw. I don't think it's particularly good for me".

What is the cost of living for ageing mothers of adults when the message from their adult offspring is clear: you are on your own. The cost of Jennifer's living is measured in isolation, emotional depletion, exile and estrangement. The cost of Kathy's, Allie's, Claire's and Sally's living is measured in isolation, financial stress, emotional distress, exile and estrangement. In the end, the cost of living for ageing mothers of adults in industrialised nuclear families is their capacity for managing the pain inflicted by the cornucopia of diminishing returns on her body and her spirit. *It hurts.* The isolation hurts. The exile hurts. The rejection hurts. The decades of using her body in the service of babies and children and families our own and not our own hurts. We are tired. We keep going. We hurt. We keep going. Those among us who have fallen into estrangement are exhausted and 'out of puff'. We keep going. Still we rise. Look into her eyes if you dare. All this – all this – is waiting down the line for the empowered middle aged, like a fully loaded train of carriages harnessed to an idling caboose. Please don't ask why ageing mothers do not discuss the situation with their adult offspring. If you have to ask, you have not been paying attention.

Who does the ageing mother and grandmother become when no-one is expecting her home? How do we measure her health, wellbeing and the cost of her living when her decisions are made from places of stress, distress, bewilderment and exclusion? How does she know herself when she can expect little engagement beyond her usefulness to others? Who is she in an era when 'mother' is judged so harshly she is trapped in a vortex, spider in a bottle of longing, loneliness and endless no-escape no-reprieve shame, judgement and unrequited love? What becomes of her enspirited body when those she has loved all her life no longer come to the door to greet her? What is the cost of living for ageing mothers who, heading into life's end game, find themselves bereft of of inclusion and with it the falling away of familial hope, care, engagement, touch, gifts, remembrance.

The displacement of the ageing mother from the hearth in the modern western nuclear family comes at the least viable time in her life, when she can least afford to be displaced. In our long-living times the process of ageing brings with it a turning to dust of all that is behind the unclanned western ageing mother until she vanishes into the cloud of that same dust. For decades we knew ourselves as the driving force at the nucleus of the all-inclusive nuclear family 'we', to find with the receding years our 'we' usurped by 'you' and then 'us-not-you'. What measure dust in the accounting for the cost of our living? In the words of the poet Emily Dickinson, *I am out with lanterns, looking for myself.*

We create our mothers just as surely as mothers create their sons and daughters. For the unpartnered or untethered ageing mother there is no ally, no witness, no champion. This too measures the cost of her living. The pearling woman, Mel, is adamant that had she had a partner her treatment inside her son's home would have been quite different. There would have been a witness to her daughter-in-law's behaviour, in which case, she said, "dinner absolutely would have been on the table, for us all". If not a direct witness, there would be someone to whom she could have reported her experience. This calling to account, either directly or by proximity, would likely have modified the daughter-in-law's behaviour. A witness, confidante, champion or ally would likely have reduced the violent backwash on Mel's body and mitigated the rupture in her relationships with her son and grandchildren.

For decades my mother had a scrap of paper tucked into her purse. It contained a line from a poem written in 1776 by David Garrick: *fellow feeling makes us wondrous kind.* A week after Caroline spoke of her longing for reprieve from the behaviour of her adult daughter, she emailed an apology she wanted me to pass on to the women with whom she had shared that moment. She was ashamed she had spoken so freely and had not 'held herself together'. In cold separation from the women who had shared her experience as the ageing mother of an adult daughter, without the warmth of 'wondrous kind', Caroline felt exposed in the world. Fellow feeling is Adler's community feeling in maturity. In a world awash with sibling-love and money, fellow feeling is lost to private logic, and is thereby incapable of sharing either love or money. We are industrialised western nations of hoarders, sibling individualists who covet heart gold as readily as cash, stockpiling it for those who need it: Ourselves.

# 5.

## Threshold Crossings

THIS BOOK IS at heart a collection of small tidings. They chronicle the hail of tiny arrows fired at the everyday living bodies of the ageing mothers of adults who commonly dwell on the fringes of modern western nuclear families. Its purpose is to celebrate our strength and our courage. Still we rise. Still we stand. Its resolve is to illuminate the experiences of ageing mothers of adults enduring the creeping estrangement of slow burn exile and to let you know your experience is not unique and it is not personal. You didn't 'do' anything. Whether or not you are buoyed by this knowledge, the fact is you are not alone on the tide receding from the hearthstone of modern western family living. You are not alone in the silence. You are not alone behind the mask through which others fail to peer. You are not the only one to wash up on the tide of her own tears.

Once recovered from the surprise we find ourselves on this shoreline, comes recognition and realisation that it was never going to be any other way for the unclanned ageing mother. Our mistake, whether blindly or wilfully, was thinking we were exempt from the nature of our times. Rather than seeking a diagnosis and further embedding ourselves in the pathogenic sibling society nightmare of modern western living, we ought turn our attentions and energies to the restoration of sanity, our own and others'.

Some years ago I watched a documentary about managing dingoes in Australia's remote grazing lands, where farmers lose lambs and calves to marauding dogs. Dingoes are fair game for farmers, who shoot to eradicate. Except on one property, where a couple was so tired of the war with dingoes they resolved to live with them. Instead of shooting to eradicate, they tithed a share of their stock to dingoes. The outcome for the tithing couple was, without foresight or expectation, the restoration of both the dingo pack and their farmland. The young dogs run riot were brought to heel by the older dogs. The pack eventually hunted only for food. The dingoes shared the waterhole with cattle. The cattle drank only when necessary, liberating the land around the waterhole from incessant trampling hooves and re-establishing plant and wildlife.

In human terms, this is a threshold crossing. The restoration of the pack is the restoration of clan, and by extension nature. The sibling young brought to heel returns ageing grandmothers to the hearth centre. In preparation for this, ageing mothers have work to do. Even though it is too late for us to benefit other than personally from our own maturing, rather than leaving behind a pre-paid funeral perhaps the sublime legacy we can leave our adult daughters and sons and their children, adult and otherwise, is the restoration of the clan and a visible rightful order of place in the scheme of things.

Our starting place might be what philosopher Phillip Goulding describes, through the mouth of the ancient Pythia, as "the sorrow beyond the shame". This quality of sorrow is a surrender to what is, the place where the wintered ageing mother of adults falls below her grief into "the void with the grief before it is eternal". Now she is ready to return to the world, to make her way back with redoubled strength. First, she must be willing to die to what was.

Filmmaker Jef Sewell observes the modern world's obsession with fictional lives (streaming) and "immortality projects" (social media) reflects the "need to be the hero in our own world". This, he says, equates to denial of death. Simone de Beauvoir tells us the natural consequence of denial of death is the turning away from the ageing and elderly in our society. Says Kingsley, "if we want to grow up and become true men and women we have to face death before we die.

We have to discover what it is to be able to slide behind the scenes and disappear".

Fortunately for us the ancient ones, those whose sacred rites survived the onslaught of western logic for a time, left tracings that show us how to do this. We know them as, in one instance, 'the Eleusinian mysteries'. Taken seriously they are rites of passage from maiden to queen, journeys through landscapes of becoming; of separation, grief and reunion; a renewal of the mother-daughter bond. They are maturing experiences that mark transitions between loss of innocence and agency, the ageing mother returned to the world as Queen of the Underworld, gatekeeper of the hidden realms, the thirteenth fairy at the party, a woman enriched with embodied transformative wisdom. She knows who she is and she knows where she belongs, and, like the thirteenth fairy, she is impenitent about it.

These rites are initiations of the maturing psyche, which is the true work of psychology. They centre around the maiden/daughter Persephone and her mother, Demeter. '*Sophe*', meaning wisdom, is the proper work of philo*sophy*, and psychology. Persephone was also known as Kore, meaning daughter, or girl. She represents a state of inner disconnection, the fallen psyche, the one who is flailing and failing to mature; the soul in exile. Demeter means mother. She represents the pure psyche, a woman in her undivided state deeply attuned to beauty, knowledge and the sacred. She is whole, her creative spirit enlivened and intact, and she is unbound by fear, ego (individualism) and socially prescribed scripts (compliance). She perceives the world with clarity and insight, giving rise to compassion, wisdom and right action. Wisdom is not vengeance. Wisdom is not polite. Wisdom demands our surrender. Wisdom will settle for nothing less than death of the heroising grasping romanticised self obsessive unmatured individual. This is what it is to be an elder. When every bone in your body sings of life's weathering. This is what our times and our families need from us. Now.

We are not Eleusinians. We are twenty-first century westerners living in times that threaten not just ourselves and our families but every living creature and lifeform on our planet. We can recreate rites that are our heritage but in reality whose depth and contextualised experience was lost to us almost two millennia ago. We can turn to the religions and spiritual teachings of other times and cultures, re-packaged and memed in deliberate obfuscation of human maturing, and become what Kingsley describes as "cultural tramps and vaga-bonds, homeless in our own land".

Or we work with what we have. And what we have are the primary feeling forces of Longing, Loneliness and Love; capacity for languaging our lives and times anew; writing as the medium through which we might undertake this demanding journey; and each other, the age-ing mothers of adults willing to find their experiences reflected in the eyes of 'wondrous kind' on the pathway leading beyond the sibling society madness that marks our times.

## The braiding forces

Early explorations of Longing, Loneliness and Love identified these powerful forces as discrete currents existent in the living human body. Here at the deep end of these explorations, recognising the indis-tinguishable feeling nature of both the existent currents and their synonymic counterparts (small 'l' longing, loneliness and love), I have come to realise that in their primal form Longing, Loneliness and Love are not separate. They are a braiding, like loosely twisted rope. They are a united, ignited, fluid force, huge and plump and soft, braid-ing its way through the nervous system, threading the dark places of blood and bone and fat and flesh in the feeling body, and from there into the world in healthy mobility, transfer and exchange.

Braid*ing*, not braided. Braiding is a verb: active, engaged, on-going. The braiding forces of Longing, Loneliness and Love are either in con-stant exchange and flow within the living human body and beyond, or they are stagnant, subjugated by wilful sibling madness to the unleashed riot of wanting, wishing, desiring, yearning, small 'l' loneli-ness and 'love' in its multitude of selective, contracted, exclusionary forms. Small 'l' longing, loneliness and love are unmatured feelings and emotions outsourced to others for redress. Like adolescent dingoes without benefit of Robert Bly's 'good mother energy', they are destructive energies unleashed and orphaned without discipline and guidance in the world.

As unmatured feeling forces, small 'l' longing, loneliness and love are scattered, in the body and the world. No-one escapes their eruptions and shatterings. Their depths of beauty and despair are alluring, an undisciplined teetering of shame and desire, blame and affection, contraction and friendship, withdrawal and exclusive belonging, silencing and engagement in the world. They are subject to sway with momentary notice, plunging a human being into the highs and lows of living, often taking others with them.

At no time in human existence have human beings not been rocked by and struggled to overcome the unmatured feeling forces. This is what maturity is. It is an overcoming of these interiorised forces. It is the disciplining of self. It is willingness and capacity to hold ourselves together in the face of fear, change and consequence. It is the maturing ability to manage emotions and sustain a steady heart in the body and in the world. The children cannot possibly learn how to do this if the sibling adults around them refuse to grow up. All the professional expertise in the world will not save you or them if we will not help ourselves.

The willingness to take action on our own behalf is foundational to the activation of the braiding forces of Longing, Loneliness and Love in the living human body. It is also the driving impulse of the wellbeing theories foundational to the ideas in this text – that health and wellbeing are an assemblage that simultaneously includes and is beyond the realm of one individual; that health and wellbeing is capacity for living in life's flow – dwelling and mobility; and that health and wellbeing are predicated on individuals, families and communities comprehending, managing and making sense of life-welt circumstances (the salutogenic sense of coherence).

Longing and Loneliness are true-north indicators of the work-in-the-world of individuals. In common pop guru parlance they *are* 'your true purpose' and 'your authentic self'. They are personal, intimate expressions of each human being. Love, on the other hand, is the centrifugal force. It is the gift in constant exchange with others through my/your body into all the world bodies, to return in kind, infinite and dynamic. Longing, Loneliness and Love are maturing braiding forces united and in flow in the feeling body, igniting healthy cycles of release and return in the world.

I have been reflecting on the letter L: longing, loneliness, love, loyalty, loss, language, living. Life words start with L. L is a cornerstone, a foundation, a point of connection. It is a right angle, strong, grounding, a form to build upon. It marks transition, change, a turning point. As a half square, it represents that which is incomplete yet forming, containing within it the invitation to wholeness. The letter L has been consistent in shape and sound for more than three thousand years, making its way through Phoenician, Greek, Etruscan, Latin, medieval and modern languages. It came to us from the Phoenician *lamedh*, meaning ox goad, staff or lash – a tool for guidance. For the Phoenicians, it directed animals. For the Hindus, it directed right action, expression and wisdom. Transposed to the context of *Mothercry*, 'right action' is the ageing mother of adults returned to the hearth; 'expression' is her voice, welcome at the hearth; 'wisdom' is that which she knows that the sibling young cannot. In a post-sibling society world that is crying out for restoration of the vertical, L is the bridge, the change in direction, our modern-day English-languaged post-Eleusinian symbol of the pathway to guidance and self mastery. L is the stable body host to the braiding forces of Longing, Loneliness and Love.

For understanding Longing we turned to available works from pre-Socratic western heritage, to the time before the logician-philosophers began dissecting and compartmentalising Life. For comprehending Loneliness we turned to mid-twentieth century scholarship, to a time before peak sibling society. To know Love, we will turn to the Sufis.

The modern westerner defines love as a panoramic nothing applied equally to children, ice-cream and movies. In its eminent form it is reserved exclusively for select people – *you, but not you*. The ancient Greeks, widely credited as being the founding fathers of western ways and knowledge, split love into varying categories, such as *eros*, fiery longing for union with another; *philia*, deep and loyal friendship and *storge*, the instinctive love that binds families. Rather than splitting hairs about love, it is the Sufi teachers and mystics to whom we will turn for understanding Love as a centrifugal force.

For the Sufis, Love is the essence of existence. It is not an emotion but a sacred fire, a divine current flowing through all creation that is neither sentimental nor possessive. From the Iraqi mystic Rābiʻa al-ʻAdawiyya we learn that Love is not transactional. Therefore, that which can be given and taken away is not Love. She identified Love as rooted in Longing and surrender, from which we might understand that Love and Longing are synergetic, and that Love is not ours to control but to concede to. The Persian mystic Fatima al-Nisaburiya regarded Love not as comfort but as transformation through life's trials, the essential meeting of the soul life in the maturing human being. The Sevillian philosopher Ibn al-ʻArabī identified all existence as rooted in Love. These understandings are illuminated by a parable attributed to the famous street mystic Shams of Tabriz, teacher of the famous poet Mevlânâ Celâleddîn-i Rûmî, himself a master and devotee of Love. Says Shams, the intellect ties people in knots and risks nothing. Love dissolves all tangles and risks everything. Love can reduce us to rubble. Treasures are found in ruins.

The intellect ties people in knots *and risks nothing*. The problem with the western mind is the western mind. The same intellect that got us into this sibling madness is never ever going to lead us out of it. We-the-west are a billion collectively powerful, intellectually limited, socially undisciplined people out of balance with life. We want what we want. We take what we want. We give to charities in noble largesse when what we have has come on the backs of those same people we claim to help. Whether it's the diamonds on our fingers or the chocolate in our bellies or eco tourism to salve our bored and self-indulgent consciences or plastic toys at Christmas or salt lamps radiating 'health benefits', everything we want comes on the backs of others: their land, their water, their air, their enspirited bodies, their families, their lives. We the west are one-eighth of the world's human population and we have everything. Yet our children are in crisis, our elderly want to die and the entire population appears to be so utterly miserable with everyday life a huge percentage of us takes pills to cope and there are not enough budgetary resources to meet growing demands for health services.

It is time for us to grow up. A quick glance at a friend's social media feed features a 'one-week course to become an ADHD coach', the opportunity to learn about the 'five most common sources of trauma in women', and a 'trauma-informed yoga' program. All are symptoms of the western mind in perpetual adolescence and susceptible to indoctrination and sway from academic thought bubbles with a marketing plan. These symptoms include Szasz's astutely observed 'living in the world' problems; Adler's private logic triumphing over community feeling; and the western mind unrooted in the heart yet obsessed with love – and this, says contemporary Sufi scholar Pia Zia Inayat Khan, is a problem. Mental function must be rooted in the living heart.

Curiously, and without intention, during the ten years I led wellbeing-through-writing programs in the Australian outback, I experienced this phenomenon directly. I had created a pair of workshops to be delivered back-to-back on the same day. The first focused on getting people started on a writing project, which for most participants was a community or family history and for others a memoir or, occasionally, a novel. At essence, the workshop's intent was unsilencing the silenced voice. Rather than opening the workshop with formal introductions, such as 'what is your name' and 'what do you do', it opened with one question: what do you love? The purpose of the question was to throw participants off the scent of terror about what lay ahead in the writing workshop. It surprised them, it bonded the circle and it was easy to answer in writing. Before names, before identity, 'what do you love', 'what lights you up', 'what makes you shine' – and no-one, not a single person, ever said they loved a material possession. Not cars, not clothes, not jobs, not computer devices, not phones, not houses, not even homes. Here's what we love: other people, music, laughter, singing and dancing, the wild world, animals, gardens, stories, creating. Incidentally, the most common reason in those same workshops for not doing these things: 'I don't have time'. Isn't that precious? The privileged west has all the things but doesn't have time for love.

The second workshop opened with a simple technique, a taster for accessing three 'intelligences' available to a human being. These 'intelligences' mirrored the slogans of our time: mind, body, heart. The first intelligence invited participants to think of a problem that was top of mind and dump what the mind had to say about it onto the page. The second invited them to close their eyes, visit the world inside their skin, and write the body's feeling response to the problem. A range of guiding questions was poured into the process while they wrote. The third intelligence invited them into their heart, to write what the feeling heart had to say about the matter. Almost without exception, the mind writing filled a page or five of blather, while the heart writing was a word or five that delivered a directive. Rather than having no idea what to do, participants realised they knew exactly what they needed to do. *You know what you need to do.* The question is, are you willing to do it? And right there is the portal for accessing the power and efficacy of writing as a health practice and the dilemma facing the western mind: it wants what it wants without sacrifice.

Paraphrasing Pia Zia Inayat Khan, for humans to be well beings mental function must be rooted in the living heart. Through this lens, the undisciplined mind, unrooted in the living heart, is subject to the vagaries of the world, to multitudes of fears and struggles.

It is perpetually in survival mode, subject to reactivity and self-aggrandisement, obsessed with 'immortality projects'. A mind rooted in the heart meets life as one body, thereby having capacity to view life from the vantage point of a whole being. Says Pia Zia Inayat Khan, "the heart provides a larger frame of guidance for a symbiotic understanding of life. Moral courage requires going beyond reactivity".

Moral courage is the mission ahead for ageing mothers of adults and grandchildren in a world in crisis.

## Longing as guide

Beneath the loud voice proclaiming 'my truth' to the world is a quieter voice, the whisper within. Whereas the 'inner self' has all the loud words she can muster to her embattled defence, the whisper within is pre-language. The whisper within is the flutter in the belly, the warm breath of 'this' on skin, the quickening of a heartbeat. The whisper within is not loud, not angry. If it has words they are few. It knows no truth but the universal. It is the quiet summons within that says, '*this*'.

The quiet 'this' is always an expression of Longing. Longing has no salve, no satisfaction in the getting, no promise of gain. Longing is an unfurling. It is its own path and its own saviour. To answer the summons within is to lay out a path on which to travel, to surrender as each step along the way reveals the next step to be taken. This is where the journey begins for the ageing mother preparing to return with redoubled strength. She answers the summons, the flutter, the warm breath, the quickening within. She surrenders to the mystery that will forever remain a mystery. *It is the step forward that matters.* As she prepares for that step forward – the preparation itself being a step forward – she likely casts about for language to describe for herself the call of soul/psyche: *What is the 'this' that haunts my living days? What is the 'this' that shows up in my dreaming?* You may or may not ever know what the 'this' is or what it will ask from you.

Longing is persistent. Longing asks for movement and rest, for dwelling and mobility. Longing demands response and presence.

Longing is not desire, wanting, wishing, yearning. Ignored or denied, Longing is corrosive. Longing always knows what to do – next; for the next moment is the only moment available to us. The shape of longing is personal, often formless, deeply felt. Longing is your private dance. Longing belongs only to you.

As Peter Kingsley writes, Longing is "a line of utter simplicity" that invites us beyond appearances into a deeper world. It opens our eyes to hidden patterns and recurring principles. In time, everything begins to speak with the voice of your Longing, revealing meaning, direction and the sacred rhythm of your Life.

Stepping towards Longing is an act of moral courage.

## Loneliness as fortification

The state of Loneliness without an objectified other is the audacious decision to 'traffic with oneself' in the body's interior, knowing there is only one other who will meet you there: Hades himself, guardian of the threshold to the Underworld. This is the unmatured maiden Psyche's demanding initiatory rite of passage, the tribulative journey through panic, fear, anguish and feelings of profound inner exile, to find treasure in the rubble and emerge as Queen of the Underworld.

This withdrawal from the world is rarely undertaken from a position of sure-footedness and certainty in the world (although the undertaker, Hades, will eventually come for the certain and the sure-footed too). Hades steals Psyche from the world, just as slow burn exile steals the ageing mother from the hearthstone of the unclanned modern western nuclear family. Mythologist Joseph Campbell observed it is not meaning we seek, but the experience of meaning. Experience is of the body. Feeling is the jurisdiction of the body. Meaning enacted through the body is the experience of meaning. Modern western women seek meaning. Loneliness is the work of meaning, *the work* of 'my true purpose', *the work* of 'my authentic life'. The choice is yours – meet Hades at the threshold, or he will steal you from the world. The willing withdrawal from the world to slide behind the scenes to disappear is anathema to the modern western individual obsessed with immortality projects. Those among us desperate for a diagnosis need take a breath and understand: Hades has already stolen you from the world. The bad news: Hades has you in hell. The good news: the decision to take a hike to the underworld has already been made for you.

There is no easy route to mastering Loneliness. It is the journey towards overcoming vast and powerful emotional interior forces. It is to 'grow up' and 'get a grip' and 'get over yourself' and 'pull yourself together' and 'get real'. It is to find Loneliness as fortification for the shattered heart of ageing mothers of adults. It is to make peace with not belonging to anyone and in return belonging to the world. It is to return to the light above, in the words of philosopher Alan Watts "unadorned, unfiltered and unafraid", liberated from the "drama of needing to be desired". It is to summon courage enough to live as the thirteenth fairy, "no longer intoxicated by romance and approval", an unpraised being for whom silence is strength, not withdrawal.

In mastering Loneliness the ageing mother of adults knows what the empowered sibling young and middle aged cannot know. She sees what they cannot see. She hears what they cannot hear. She is wisdom personified in the maturing ageing body. Returned to the light, wintered and well, belonging in and of and to the world, the ageing mother of adults in the modern western nuclear family makes herself ready to begin the work of restoration of the clan.

Mastering Loneliness is a supreme act of moral courage.

## Love as sustenance

Love as a centrifugal force wants nothing for itself. It is enlivening. It is fuel and flame for the journey of Life. In the words of the Sufi poet Rûmî Love is "the cause and effect of all things". It is the fire of creation. It 'rages against individuality'. It is not a comforting force. Love heralds community feeling over private logic. As a state of being it is hard-earned and hard won, even though, paradoxically, we need do nothing to ennoble this state but concede to moral courage and surrender what does not and never did matter. In maturity, Love renders us capable of distinguishing seduction from surrender, guile from Grace. Love is a gateway into being a whole being, capable of enduring the outer reaches of human experience and feeling. Love is life, as it is. Loyalty is the blood of Love.

The maturing braiding forces of Longing and Loneliness root Love in the world. It is here we meet the paradox of self-possession as antithesis and adversary to individualism. Raking through pre-Socratic tracings of the ancients, Kingsley provides a clear distinction between the small 'l' love of individualism's obsession and Love as a braiding force. For Kingsley, small 'l' love is the territory of the unmatured psyche trapped in perpetual maidenhood. Liberation from entrapment, the transformation of maiden to Queen, is made possible when we "die before we die". To descend, willingly or otherwise, is to tumble into the dark interior of our being, to burn in the fires of interior conflict for the clear purpose of disentangling attachments. It is to return to the world above to cycle through maturing states of sacred, unshakeable peace. This is the empowered silence of restraint. It is the silence of the ageing woman who has learned to brew fire in her belly. It is the self-possessive silence of engaged self-alignment. This unshakeable peace is what the Sufis call Love, 'the pearl of great price' to be found in the depths of darkness. To blame others for distresses of soul, for the worried well to take a pill and seek a diagnosis rather than travel through the dark, is to broker trouble. It is to refuse the journey and with it the advantages of returning with redoubled strength. It is to settle for all the faces of suffering and renege on Life.

> *There in the lucky dark,*
> *none to observe me, darkness far and wide –*
> *no sign for me to mark,*
> *no other light, no guide*
> *except for my heart – the fire, the fire inside!*
> St John of the Cross

*She bore life's empty pack*
*as gallantly as if the East*
*were swinging at her back.*
*Life's empty pack is heaviest,*
*As every porter knows –*
*in vain to punish honey,*
*it only sweeter grows.*
Emily Dickinson

It wasn't just the ancients who left us tracings. While neither Emily nor John were ageing mothers of adults, like myriad others over the centuries they have travelled this way before us. *It only sweeter grows.*

Says Kingsley:

> "We're afraid of loss, and yet it's through what we lose that we're able to find what nothing can take away from us. We run from sadness and depression. But if we really face our sadness we find it speaks with the voice of our deepest longing; and if we face it a little longer we find that it teaches us the way to attain what we long for."

The Longing *is* the path.

Whereas Longing promises no allies, and Loneliness no witness, the primal feeling force of Love offers sustenance for this intensely solo journey towards self as straw made gold. Moral courage asks more from the unclanned ageing mothers of adults than performing or masking grief on social media. It asks more than sustaining imposed and self-imposing silencings among family and in the world, and this includes relying on auto-text, emojis, bitten lips and Valium to communicate with the empowered sibling daughters and sons we raised and the partners they married. Moral courage asks us to be brave, to trust our place in the scheme of things even when that scheme is actively exclusionary. It invites us to stare down the over-exerted young and middle aged and take our place as the thirteenth fairy at the sibling princess's party. It requires we find our voice rooted in the living heart.

Moral courage is the grail awaiting ageing mothers of adults in the modern western nuclear family. The braiding forces of Longing, Loneliness and Love are guidance, fortification and sustenance for the surrender of assailable sadness, as we 'slide behind the scenes and disappear' in order to return with redoubled strength and restore the vertical spine to modern western industrialised families.

## Writing as maturing practice

The process of writing as a maturing practice threads small 'l' longing, loneliness and love through a series of concurrent processes, thereby meeting shame, developing trust and coming home in the body and in the world. To enter into this process is to cultivate the promise of the maturing braiding forces of Longing, Loneliness and Love. Writing creates opportunities to evolve our feelings and the words we give our feelings. It helps us find our own words, living human words that reject the readymade slogans of the mental health industry, its wellness industry counterparts and their clever marketeers and ad men.

Words have power. Through the faint tracings left to us from Parmenides, Kingsley says, "words aren't mere descriptions. They are living seeds, intended to be planted and cultivated in the body". The clever ad men know this. Finding our own words restores our language, our voice and our agency as we move about the world as we know ourselves to be. This is the unspoken body finding new language for feeling and for living in the world. This is the languaged 'authenticity' desired by western women.

Writing is a solo journey. It is itself a living metaphorical underworld. Many a brave writer has found treasures within that wrought havoc and severe reckoning along the way. With courage enough to pursue the maturing braiding force of Longing through writing, once the unfurling of shame has begun, ageing mothers of adults will meet minefields of small 'l' loneliness. This is where the maturing work of Loneliness begins. Whether small 'l' or capital L, Loneliness is marked by the absence of a witness. The page is your witness.

Laura addressed the power of this witnessing directly. When trouble strikes her day, she knows she must "go to the pages":

> "The pages are essential. They unpack the anguish I'm feeling about the dynamics in the family. They give me a completely different spotlight to throw onto my racing feelings. If I do three pages I've unpacked whatever I'm struggling with, enough for insights to come in. Without writing, I cannot reach those insights. It brings more than relief, it brings architecture, it brings direction, it brings assertiveness, it brings acceptance. I can build a room of one's own out of that mess of emotion, a space I can stand in that is clarity. In the end, if I can't understand the meaning of my life, I can at least understand the meaning of my day."

Wellbeing-through-writing and rumination in writing are not the same thing. Novelist Elif Shafak described words as like "eggs about to hatch". There is simultaneous wonder and caution in her sentiment. For instance, as the pen leads Laura through what she is 'unpacking', she is clearly avoiding melancholy and rumination in her writing. We know this by what she revealed about her process – three pages and it's done. To do otherwise is to lose oneself in the minefields of past wounds and hurts and shames and blames. To do otherwise is to miss the point and fall prey to contemporary monsters and their endless wanderings in the underworld with no promise of return.

One antidote to rumination is the three intelligences outlined earlier in this chapter: 1. dump it on the page; 2. find the words in the feeling body; 3. let psyche, soul, heart have its say about the matter. Three pages. Dump it and move on. Writing is soul work. To stew in the past is to ruminate, to tumble through Hades' gate and have no idea you're even there.

Theologian Rowan Williams tells us we are "entering a world in which we need new verbal resources to cope". Verbal resources are imperative to languaging the maturing braiding forces of Longing, Loneliness and Love in the living body. Writing is a means for discovering and recovering those verbal resources. What does the maturing force of Longing feel like in the living body? What does the maturing force of Loneliness feel like in my living body? What does the maturing force of Love feel like in your living body? To explore in writing is to find words and language for this radical act of self possession. Writing gives us words to traffic with ourselves, to consciously mature the braiding forces. Ultimately, regardless of how strong the ageing mother of adults is feeling, it is words and verbalised language she needs to make her way with agency in her family and in the world.

Essayist Maria Popova writes "every act of communication is an act of tremendous courage … even the warmest intention can be met with frost." Frosted warm intentions speak to the exhausted, wintering hearts of ageing mothers of adults. Finding language for the experiences in her feeling body will restore her spirit and thaw the heart, offering grist enough to move forward with emerging, growth-full courage and trust in the world. For ageing mothers of adults who seek genuine maturity, worthy hard-won transformational wisdom that is the spinning of self from straw to gold, writing is both pathway and process for undertaking this radical act of languaged self possession, to 'die before we die' as they enter Hades' <u>western</u> gate.

Almost nobody is truly born to mysticism. The west has not the discipline. Weekend workshops and online programs filtered through the 'white women's wellness industry' are at best indulged comfort offering food for thought and bursts of insight. The work of true mysticism is annihilating. The wellbeing-through-writing process mirrors the journey of the human psyche as its intersects with longing/Longing, loneliness/Loneliness, love/Love. It highlights the realities of the kinds of transformation accessible to modern western women who are willing to show up for themselves. The journey is demanding, insightful, sustaining, life-changing. It will deliver presence-enough, and develop the foundational courage and trust it takes to enliven the senses, live daily from this place and *keep going*. And this will deliver transformation enough for the price most will be willing to pay in one lifetime.

Moral courage is Bly's 'good mother energy' and 'good mother energy' is in our time a state of radical self possession. Ageing mothers of adults who seek to rise above sibling society madness and live from this radical state must be willing to recover their energy systems and prevent further exhaustion. They must be willing 'pull themselves together' and 'get real'. The over-exerted over-empowered middle aged and young cannot know their place in the scheme of things if we do not return ourselves to our place in the scheme of things. And our place, lest we forget, is the hearth centre. This is a process of 'becoming'. The maturing forces of Longing, Loneliness and Love are our guides, our fortifications and our sustenance. As are other ageing mothers of adults on this revolutionary path.

Before becoming, unbecoming.

## The omphalos of unbecoming

Ageing mothers of adults who seek voice, agency and rightful place of belonging at the modern western nuclear family hearth have work to do. That work is a reckoning. It begins with a showdown, a face-off with a double act of confusing and conflicting forces that have converged in our times at peak power in the bodies of ageing mothers of adults in modern western nuclear families. The first is rigid social prescriptions about who, what, how and where women should be. The second is the modern individualised sibling society self who wants it all and refuses to grow up. These are no small forces. The first is the result of at least two millennia's worth of socialised pressure piling onto the enspirited bodies of ageing women, non-compliance with which could and still can cost a woman her life. The second is ageing women's collusion with the fantasy promises peddled by marketeers and profiteers during the century that saw the rise of the west's contemporary monsters. Facing off with these forces is a supreme act of moral courage and heralds change for everyone in an ageing woman's orbit.

The shattered hearts of ageing mothers of adults will find redress not in therapy, but in attention to soul. Poet Walt Whitman observed the "body electric" reveals the soul. The body electric is *sentire*, an Italian word that means at once to see, to hear and to feel. Literature professor Robert Harrison describes sentire as "the most wondrous word I know in any language". Sentire is what ageing mothers of adults are cultivating and surrendering to as they step forward for their Longing and prepare to enter the underworld through Hades' western gate.

Mythologist Joseph Campbell said, "life hurts. We don't say no to life". Maturity is the enspirited body whose soul has, in the words of psychiatrist Thomas More, "really lived and is complicated and deep". This is work of deep repair. It is the work of recovering the senses. The transmutation of loneliness to Loneliness as a braiding force is the point at which, paraphrasing philosopher John McGraw, a human being's capacity for intimacy is commensurate with her ability to suffer Loneliness. That commensurateness is Love. McGraw might well have been addressing Love directly when he pointed out that conditions of loneliness incorporate anxiety, shame, guilt, sadness; that self-renewal and serenity are dependent upon finding a home within oneself beyond reach of the roar of everyday existence; and that the greatest likelihood for fulfilling this condition is a home outside oneself, through, for example, unconditional family love that makes possible a home for all in the outside world.

Isn't that sublime? *Love that makes possible a home for all in the outside world.*

As human beings our source of belonging is inside the family, and whilst humans may find or construct versions of family elsewhere, they do so in exile from family. With or without our consent we are rooted in family. When the family turns on us, there is nothing but what we can find from the remainder table. McGraw defined the possibilities of homecoming as qualities of intimacy such as "attentiveness, affiliation, affection, attachment, devotion, loyalty, care, trust, confidentiality, sympathy, empathy and, above all, love" – all of which empowered middle aged sibling society individuals demand for themselves, yet deny 'mother'. It is a lonely business being the left mother. If she does not have your loyalty, you and she both may consider her abandoned.

In an everyday way, as the twenty-first century marches on, life is as mundane as it ever was. Life is repetitive and, put bluntly, it is boring. To live as an adult is to endure routines of housework, other people, shopping, and so on. In our times, we do this whilst witnessing the stellar lives of other people performed in digital rapture. In between come the polished ads, the outrage and the disaster porn, depending on your individualised algorithmic bubble of doom. At the time of writing, every feeling body in the world is under assault, if not from digital media then from bombs and other manmade disasters such as extreme poverty, drought and displacement. Yet the great challenge for the well-fed worried well in the west is staying sane inside the mundanity of everyday life. *We deserved so much more.*

The antidote to this madness-making is the soul driven life. The goal of soul, says More, is not 'the perfect life, a successful life, the most smooth-functioning life' (it's still boring). More tells us to focus instead on the "ordinary and intimate" aspects of life: other people, home, personal history, nature. He urges us to "talk long into the night" and "enjoy insights, rather than taking another course to acquire more information". Friendship, in other words. Friendship and poetry before therapy. Kingsley reinforces this by observing "we have plenty of room in our lives for knowledge and data, for learning and information, amusement and entertainment; but not for wisdom".

Wisdom is the work of the soul. To tend the soul is to act for Longing. The process of maturing the braiding forces insists you put down the phone and forego fantasy lives. Wisdom requires becoming, and becoming requires unbecoming. Solitude is imperative to unbecoming. To step into regular periods of solitude is to slide behind the scenes and disappear. This ought not be so hard for western women, who are already hankering to slide behind the scenes and disappear with every Bali retreat, every spa, every holiday that promises to *take me away from all of this.* Unbecoming is the work of the soul. Dying before we die is the work of the soul. There is no dying before you die sipping cocktails before a massage on a tropical beach at sundown no matter how much you paid for that transformational retreat.

Ours is the first generation of women to genuinely 'have time'. That we fill it with the white noise of 'crazy busy' is, in the parlance of our times, a 'lifestyle choice', and it is quite literally driving us crazy. Every single generation of non-wealthy women before us, and that is just about every woman in the family line right back up the line, had work to do that drove them from the pre-dawn hours until well after sundown. There was neither time nor inclination for a diagnosis. Modern western women have machines to do the work for them. There is almost nothing left to do for ourselves that cannot be bought or piled into a machine. And so we turn our attentions to 'healing', the modern woman's wellness obsession that cannot deliver what we seek – reprieve from life. A pill. A diagnosis. A therapist. None of which will address the root cause of the problem, down there in the underworld – discontentment of soul. Understand there is only so far the intellect can take us. Always it will lead to the gateway of mystery. Writing is soul work. Maturing is soul work. Mystery is soul work. There is work to do.

Rather than scroll the lonely evening through, put down the phone and walk circles around the house if you must until the unstimulated restless panic subsides and the channel of the embodied mind can open. Breathe. Come inside your skin. Reach for a poet or a pen, make way for reflection, create the conditions for inspiration, original thought and the possibilities of sentire. If it's a warm evening take the poet and the pen to the verandah and sit under the stars. In solitude. If it's cold, stay inside and light candles in the dark. In solitude.

In solitude we might read, write, listen, think, reflect. In solitude we might know ourselves, beyond reach of headlines and outrage and the performative lives of others.

You want your 'authentic' self, here she is. She is Persephone, vanished in the underworld, journeying through 'the lucky dark', getting real, 'bearing life's empty pack', pulling herself together, filling her skin with her own born nature, growing up. She is Demeter, bewildered, shattered and enraged as she searches for the missing daughter in the world, in service to the daughter's soul finding its way through the darkness of the underworld. Says More, surrendering to this journey is "a way of finding our own depths and even our own darkness, without cutting ourselves off from the maternal guidance within ourselves that keeps us in life and in community".

To unbecome is to unravel, to release one's grip on status or place in the world, to forego role and identity, to drift with the tide and wash up on the distant shore. It is to endure myriad confrontations with shame. It is to become adept at recognising the obstacle is the way. It is to not-know for a very long time. Undertaking (that word again) this work by entering Hades' western gate will be demanding, but not too rough. Life will go on, pretty much as normal, except the ageing mother's soul will be enlivened. She is becoming the mature soul, non-negotiable and in play. She knows she will not win the war, yet she is accomplished at selecting her battles and living as a disappeared woman between times.

## The solitudinal step

To step into solitude is to step in the true work of thinking. Hannah Arendt described thinking as an intensely inward, solitary activity, something that unfolds within a private world, "a soundless dialogue between me and myself, the two in one". She observed that rather than being a cerebral activity, "one must think with the body and the soul or not think at all". Whilst true thinking requires solitude, its reality, its moral force, its accountability in the world, is effective only when it is embodied through speech and action before others. Effective thinking, wrote Hannah, is that in which "the two (me and myself) who carry on the thinking dialogue be in good shape, that the partners be friends". In other words, the ageing mother of adults who enters into solitude with genuine intent to thinking as a maturing practice must first 'get into good shape'. She must purge the terrorists on the inside, the riotous inner voices destabilising her health and wellbeing. She must cultivate instead the conditions of interior friendship between 'the two in one', to prepare herself for the learned practice of thinking as an embodied soul. Solitude is the condition that prescribes the learning.

In prescribing the conditions for thinking, Hannah described conditions for maturing the braiding forces of Longing, Loneliness and Love through will, practice and discipline. To pick up the pen in the spirit of wellbeing-through-writing practice is to meet 'the two in one', 'me and myself', in the space where mind, breath and body convene.

Through the experiential journey of surrender to the emergent braiding forces of Longing, Loneliness and Love, in concurrent interdependent cyclical fractal creation, the ageing mother of adults writes herself home. She does so not to indulge the interior self, but to 'think with body and soul' to recover her whole self, to liberate her soul from the legions of the bewildered and the harsh impositions of others. These underworld journeys transform desire and wanting to Longing through actioning the whisper within. They transform loneliness to Loneliness through solitude and the willingness to trade the cluttered mind for thinking. They navigate the underworld of unbecoming to burst into the light of becoming, there to meet the challenges of spinning small 'l' love to Love. Self as straw made gold.

It is important to note that stepping into solitude for ageing mothers of adults who spend their lives alone in their homes presents profoundly different challenges to women who are partnered and must work around another, or others. The untethered and unpartnered ageing mother of adults may be justifiably terrified of yet more silence. The partnered ageing mother is more likely to be challenged by adjustments in interpersonal dynamics in her home, so as to claim uninterruptable time and space for thinking in solitude. These are challenges of impotence for the partnered and isolation for the unpartnered and untethered. Hannah warned impotence and isolation "have always been characteristic of tyrannies", and can result in "the fundamental inability to act at all".

Hannah of course was referring to political regimes of the early twentieth century. Her observations are equally astute in reference to the familial structures of the modern west nearly a century later. The behaviour of adult children in the sibling society west may well be described as psychic tyranny, wielded over the spirits of ageing mothers and grandmothers in slow burn exile. Whether untethered, unpartnered or partnered, ageing mothers of adults are prone to the loneliness of family uprootedness and superfluousness. Said Hannah, to be uprooted means "to have no place in the world recognised and guaranteed by others" and to be superfluous means "not to belong to the world at all". *When we do not exist for those we love, we do not exist.* This point is echoed through the dry bones of time by the ancient philosopher Zarathustra, who turned to the sun and asked, 'You great star, what would your happiness be if you had not those for whom you shine?' A sibling society obsessed with self-happiness may well ask the question of itself. The following extracts from Leanne's journal during "the worst years" are a sublime illustration of the feeling nature of the pain of uprootedness and superfluousness to which Hannah was referring:

> *I am invisible. I trust no-one. I am a woman alone in the world. I will become my mother. I will be all she ever wanted for me. My heart is bitter, ready to strike. I fall into a pit of self loathing. I do not recognise myself in the mirror, pale and stricken. I must release myself from the worst of me, the ugliest, most unloveable, most unworthy for goodness, most filthy, vile sewer self. My daughters shatter me. Best I deal with the dead, because to them I owe everything.*

Such are the voices that risk rising in reflective solitude, in magnificently monstrous, bewildering, impotent, superfluous, isolated, splendid terror. Tiny arrows that bring a woman down. It is the voice of the languaged feeling body of one ageing mother of adults and grandmother of adults as she burned in the underworld. She is reliant on the 'maternal guidance within herself' to 'keep her in life and in community', to lead her through the unbearable sadness of being. She reaches for the mother she failed and the ancestors left too long without proper tribute. And she rises. We rise. We will rise. We find 'wondrous kind'. A nation of thirteenth fairies on the rise. We find our voices. We return to the world above ground. We find sure footing in the world. We cry with those who find their way to us. We roar with the wild, windswept laughter of ageing women. We root ourselves in moral courage. From unbecoming, becoming.

Last night I dreamed I was lying on the bed beside my grandmother. I felt something on my hand. In my mind's eye I checked where my arms were, then glanced down at my hand. My grandmother's hand, warm, was placed gently on top of my hand. It signalled a moment of return, up and down the family line.

## Before therapy, friendship

Maturity is a lifetime's work. It is to embody the important distinction between self possession and individualism. It is to experience life as it is rather than made to order to suit the shifting sands of today's 'mytruth'. We might begin by disciplining the great troubling of the worried well in our times – 'feeling unsafe'. We might examine the radical idea that 'feeling' unsafe is not the same as 'being' unsafe. We might learn the distinction between fears expressed as awful feelings and truly unmanageable experiences that need public health resources to cope.

Before therapy, friendship. *Friendship*. Friendship has words. It has room for speaking words. Friendship's renewal in our times requires visits to the underworld, away from contemporary monsters that have reframed friends as digital avatars and rendered it unsafe to speak freely. It requires listening without resorting to the therapists' tools of trade. Friends interrupt. Friends laugh inappropriately. Friends nod sagely only when they are not analysing you. Friends tell you you're talking rubbish. Friends let you find your way with your words. Friends don't take notes. Friends commiserate. Friends tell you to grow up. Friends grow up with you. It is at great personal risk modern western women speak freely and openly to 'friends' in our time, and this is a tragedy we can place squarely at the feet of communication data generators such as emojis, autotype and social media 'stories' that have no past, present or future, require zero reflection, connect no(actual)body and are gone in a blink to be replaced by the next blink and the next blink and the one after that and so on until … we put the phone down.

Put down the phone. Risk solitude. Make room for thinking. Cultivate a state of 'radical indifference'. Meg's 'change of heart', Alice's 'out of puff', my mother's withdrawal of enlivened interest traded for the battle shield of 'kind', can all be redefined as 'indifference that hurts'. These states speak to the shattered heart in retreat. There is a vast distinction between this state and what I propose to be a desired state of radical indifference among modern western ageing mothers of adults in slow burn exile. These qualities of radical indifference include the enspirited body disentangled from impositions and ensnarements of suffering; capacity for thoughtful solitude; the courage to be useful determined not by the wanting shattered heart that will take crumbs from the nuclear family remainder table, but by the song of an ageing mother's soul. Whether or not the ageing mother is included matters not. Strong of soul she will insert herself at the hearth. She knows her place at the centre of things. Not included yet strong of soul, she will disappear into the hallowed halls of self possession and watch, not from the sidelines but from the centre. Sentire. She has sharp eyes and wildly open senses. Nothing escapes her. Sentire. The soul driven ageing mother of adults picks her battles.

She prioritises what she loves. She has all the time in the world for what she loves, knowing the braiding force of Love will take care of the rest. Matured Love is the bridge between indifference-that-hurts and the sacred unshakeable peace of radical indifference. Thus begins the work of transformation of private logic to community feeling.

For if not us, then who?

## Restoration of the vertical and return of the pan-horizontal gaze

Wisdom is inseverable from moral courage. Respect for hard-won wisdom demands the return of the vertical gaze and expansion of the horizontal gaze beyond the mirrored sibling faces of peers all the way to the ever-renewing horizon. The pan-horizontal gaze. *Horizontal* – land, people, forests, oceans, creatures, bones, the grand welt in view, inclusive and impossible to ignore. Citing Carl Jung, Peter Kingsley tells us 'don't look forward to the future too much, unless you fail to hear the dead'. By which he means the ancestors. The above and the below. The vertical switch is an urgent imperative for the restoration of modern western industrialised families. This is made possible by resurrection of reverence for elders, ancestors, soul and underworld, placed on the high mantel of life.

Living is hard. It is not 'mother' or 'grandmother' you have issues with, it is life itself. None of us knows what we're doing here. Nothing more profound and helpful has been written about this in the last two thousand years that wasn't already written or understood in the two thousand years before that. Our task is to make peace with life. Phenomenologically speaking, the braiding forces of Longing, Loneliness and Love are a lifeline for the ageing mothers of adults. They are our lifeforce, our strength and our forward momentum. They fortify our courage. They are our source and sustenance in recovery from life's fusillade of tiny arrows.

Through the maturing braiding forces we will wriggle free from the contemporary monsters and their grip on our lives and our language, our minds and our mothers, our souls and our offspring. We will stop posting the words and ideas of people we will never know – and pause, creating opportunities to seek, speak and write our own words. We will turn our backs on the cults of self-improvement, forgoing the power of the Americans to shape us in the image of their own pathologies. We will rise above the debilitating power of adult children to shame and blame. For they have forgotten they were loved. More than this, they have forgotten how much they were loved. Our shame is the font of our wisdom. We write to remember who we are. We write to remind them who they are. We write to mobilise our soul in the service of clan and clanned communities.

Longing is the path. Loneliness is the fortification of trust in and along the way. Love is the fuel and the fire, sustenance and warmth for the solitudinal journey whilst keeping good company on life's tidal shore. Through writing we lay down our restless discontent to cultivate and mature the braiding forces in the feeling body. We develop the courage we need to inquire into the heart of another. We listen with soft hearts. We rise, we overcome, we claim, we return home.

Sentire.

The enspirited bodies of ageing mothers of adults do not have a monopoly on enduring legacies of pain. Even so, their longevity in this space is an exemplar of the raw material from which wisdom is won. For all our sakes, the exile and assault on 'mother' in the modern west must stop. Your mother is not your enemy. Nor is she yours to judge. You have everything to thank her for, and know this: she is, and has ever been, the only person in the entire world who has never taken her eyes off you. Turn around. In her living body *is* your joy and your meaning. She is what life asks from you. She is the cost of your living. She is life in vertical procession. She is your gift, in sublime return.

# 6.

## Campfire: The omphalos of the motherline

A T THE PRADO Museum in Madrid there is a life-size statue of an old woman with sharp features and flowing robes. She is roughly seated as two small children lean into her knees, captivated by the face that speaks to them. A crow, symbol of justice, memory, warning and wisdom, messenger between worlds, carks whispers at her shoulder, its left wing a protective halo around the curve of her head. She is cast in black bronze. The polished black throws strange light and shadows. She is grounded, immovable. Books and texts lie scattered at her feet. Nothing about this statue is incidental. Everything about this statue contains the point and the purpose and the spirit of this book.

I am writing my granddaughter home. This entire explorative exposition is for the beloved child now woman grown. I am writing for her visitations in the dreaming end of night, and the unchanging naturalness of love unthwarted, for love that is thwarted cannot be love. I am writing for the lost and the found, for the missing and the strong. I am writing for the mysteries and the paradoxes and the black holes of sacred time. I am writing for Love that warbles on and on and on, heart songs for the ages. I am writing for the threads that remain when the leaving is done. For the golden light of the yet unwritten. For who we are when our name is unspoken.

I am writing for the remembered in the bodies of the grandmothers, gone-not-gone. I may never see my granddaughter again, yet I see her every day and some nights in the visitations. Always, there is mutual acknowledging of the bond, sometimes a hug or a rising together from deep waters. Always she lets me know, sometimes explicitly: 'not yet'. An unclanned woman of no-longer-useful relevance to my adult children, or grandchildren, I am alone in my seeking of place in the world as my granddaughter is alone in hers. Thus I have been stalking the fracturings of the modern western industrialised family through the omphalos of the ageing mothers of adults, and doing what is left to me to do: write the children and mothers most beloved home.

I know why old people tell repetitive stories. The same stories, over and over. Sometimes within moments of the same story being told, around they go again. I'm sure there are bio-analytical and psychoanalytical explanations for this, rooted in the *x causes y* commonwealth of scientific reason. Here is a parallel explanation: that human beings are ancestrally coded to pass on wisdom to the ones they know they will be leaving. We the civilised west understand and even revere this practice among indigenous peoples. We the civilised west are busy, too busy to understand our old people are passing on their wisdom too. Only we don't see it as wisdom, having lost our capacity for listening to repetitive stories uncloaked in symbolism. No mystery there. We are too busy to linger in the echo of the unmystical ages.

In the west, self-importance has us on the run. We are no longer listening. Besides we've heard that story before. That 'story', that endless repetitive litany, is the vertical family chronicle encoded into which is everything you need to know to pass on to the adults to come that you birth, and your offspring birth, so they may pass it on to the adults they are yet to birth. That story is not the romanticised 'wisdom' the unclanned horizontal individualists ascribe to and romanticise about 'the elders'. It is so much more. *Yes I think I'm so wise.* And to whom will she sing her chronicles when no-one in the family line is genuinely interested in the living ageing woman who is their mother and grandmother, let alone recognise the ageing mother is soon to become ancestor.

A long, long time ago, human groups sat around campfires as a regular part of every day. Some still do, though not many. Not so long ago we sat on verandahs whiling away the evening. Some still do, now not so many. A long, long time ago … the elderly had a job to do and they have that job still. There is an urgency in the old to pass on the 'story', an unnecessarily small word for a gargantuan task. In the prime of my ageing status I am beginning to feel that urgency. Who will we become, and I do not mean our small nuclear disasters, who will the whole western we become now we are no longer able to discern the message from the symbol, which is to say unable to extract the wisdom from the litany of ordinary names and faces and places of whom the old ones speak, and can no longer identify values and warnings in the trials and triumphs knitted into the fabric of the family lineage. She is teaching you how to walk the fine line. He is showing you where your worth resides. They are reminding you that you belong to an unbroken chain of human beings born of Earth and it would be a mistake to forget to remember not only that you know this, but you are bound to it and you have an obligation to it. They are teaching you how to transmit your songline, and letting you know that your time around the campfire that no longer exists is coming and it will be here all too soon and here, my loves, here are your stories lest you forget and lose your way in the world.

The songline chronicles of the old ones are meant to be told over and over and over and over. *This is how we know who we are.* They are programming us. Coding us with the wisdom of the ancients that has rattled through living time into her body now to be transmitted through your living body. Only we no longer have the campfire, or the will for a campfire, or, if we do, we do not have 'time' to sit idly in the night listening to the repetitive stories of the old ones beneath the wonder of a wandering night sky to remind us of our place in the scheme of things.

I ask you, what is lost when the stories that ought to be told over and over are no longer told? What is lost now we have outsourced our stories to the profiteers and marketeers and the digital media oligarchs. Television. Movies. Podcasts. Gamers. Politicians. Economists. Ad men. The stories of others, so much more exciting than our own. What is lost when we look to our peers for guidance, forgetting or wilfully ignoring the elders who will tell us what we wish to neither hear nor heed?

Mothers look into the eyes and hearts of our daughters and are reminded of ourselves at that age. Our daughters look at us and think they never, ever want to be like us. And yet it was the raising of them that created us, the one they do not want to be. It was the breaking of our bodies that gave them life. She is your creation as surely as you are hers. It is she who bears alone the overwhelming physical pain of her isolation, on your behalf. You need her. She is your reflection. You reject her. You are nothing without her. She is *La Tradición*, the statue in the Prado museum.

This book has been written for the no-words mothers. It is written for the women left alone at the end of mothering time. It heralds caution to the mothers of young children and young adults, and grandmothers of small children: the gremlins are lurking in the shadows, just around the corner, aided and abetted by our collusion with the peddlers and profiteers of the mental health and digital media industries. In the modern industrialised western nuclear family this story is coming for us all. Depending on your purchasing power, and the grip the contemporary monsters have on your family, its impact is a matter of time and degrees.

There are multitudinous aides to health and wellbeing for the well-fed worried well who are willing to recover their senses, thereby freeing up valuable community resources for those who truly need them: eat less, move more, drink water, save sugar and alcohol for special occasions, wander, forgo stimulants for sleep, spend time in nature, visit friends, no screens after dark, take your time. Sentire. Breathe. Listen. Watch. Practice wayfinding through writing. Develop moral courage and embodied wisdom through the maturing braiding forces of

Longing, Loneliness and Love. Make way for genuine engagement with other beating hearts. Come out of hiding so others can come out of hiding too. Step into the world as you know yourself to be. I can only know my words when they mix with your ears and your words. Like you, every woman who speaks she speaks for the first time. When she speaks she is wayfinding. Life is a harp. With room for wayfinding her words, today she plays G, tomorrow a symphony. Practice lending her your ears. Practice receiving her words into your body. Leave her words alone. Protect her vulnerabilities. Let her speak for herself. Learn trust enough to speak for yourself.

Trust begins in the feeling body. How the ageing mother of adults holds her body can determine the emotions she feels. Before the story, the feeling. Rest in the quiet interior of your feeling body. Be guided by the feeling body. Learn to language the feeling body in writing. Wisdom is learned through the feeling body. Insight is not change. It is the recalibrated feeling body that interacts change. A woman who can language deep feeling in writing is a woman on the rise. The mental health industry, ruled by sibling society individuals and their too-tiny families, has forsaken, foregone or forgotten what the body has not. The body knows. The body remembers.

This journey is too big for the ageing mother who has not yet faced her demons and lost. Contrary to her belief she 'doesn't know what to do', she does know what to do – she doesn't want to do it. She knows she is waiting for a better option, one that is pleasing and asks nothing hard or challenging or difficult from her. We are here when she is ready. Ageing mothers of adults on the rise, we know what we need to do, to save us all. For all our bleating about 'women in power', we are a society that rejects women of power. We are here. We know who we are. We are the ones who know the difference between the mask and maturity. We are La Tradición!

As we make good headway into the twenty-first century, we are living a wide-ranging narrative of dispossession and crisis, a great diorama of change and reckoning, of displacement, dispossession, disconnection, disillusionment. Some of us will say it has ever been this way. Some will say times are worse than they have ever been. Some will say we have forgotten who we are. What does that even mean? *We have forgotten who we are.* Indigenous cultures know what it means. They are teaching us every time they make a land rights claim. Grandmothers and grandfathers too old to run know what it means. It was in their eyes when they stood on the shoreline waving the big ships away, carrying with them the yet unborn from the homeland, knowing they were destined to be forgotten with no-one to come after them to tend the bones in their charge. The old ones in the modern west know what that means when they remembered too late to pay homage to the old ones while they were living. It's there in the desperation on their breath, as they struggle to remember the stories they are obligated to tell the rest of us who are not listening.

Home, friends, is where the bones are. *That's what that means.*

Home is where we are rooted in the land. Home is where the heart is and making a new home still leaves your heart a long, long way from home. Home is where the hearth is. Home is where we *know* we belong. Home is our sanity and our rest and our peace of mind. It is not a house. It is not ambition or stolen dreams or privilege or mine-by-right. Home is where we belong and where we belong is where our people lie in Earth and walk yet upon Earth. Those of us born to new nations in old countries were liberated from the old ways, unshackled from customs heavy with the weight of obligation to the past and set free from responsibility and tradition. We created lives and nations that settled on ancient ground like shiny alien cities might descend on empty land. We chopped and shot and bulldozed and carved the world anew according to the desperation of our circumstances, the whims of the moment or the power available to us. Our homes did not rise from Earth to return to Earth as they did and still do in the old countries. Our orchards are not inherited from the ones who came before, ours to nurture for the generations to come. Our lives are not beholden to the ones who came before but are our own, individual and free, to create as we will without guidance, restrictions and the wisdom that was ours to inherit by right from the first mother and to pass on in our turn.

How's that working out for us?

In her ageing and elderly years, my mother spoke repetitively about her mother and her father, her grandmother and her grandfather. As I make ready to recite my own mother's lifesong I realise my mother's repetitive tellings of the family chronicles began after her parents were gone. With the arrival of responsibility for the family tellings rising from my bones, yet to be voiced, I am haunted by the viscerality of what she was speaking to those of us not-listening. Her lifesongs, our lament. Her silencing, our failure to tend the omphalos of the motherline while she was living. Without the clan we are mortally wounded in spirit. We must – we must – lift our gazes from the mythmakers' pied piping screen magic and take up residence in the world we actually live in.

Perhaps in the end we the ageing mothers of adults are in awe of what it is to birth and grow adults. We loved them as babies, oh how we loved our babies. We loved them as children, oh how we loved the children. We admire them as adults and are thrilled by the wonder of their existence, eventually to find the return gaze is mired in dreadful fault and into the silencing romp shame and exile and the heartrending realisation that *they will not love us*. All of what they loathe in us can be found in the efforts we made to ensure their survival in a world inhospitable to women and children.

The day you realise your mother was not and never was your enemy is the day your heart breaks for the last time. Look up. Look out. Look down. You are loved, deeply. Regardless of what she did or what you think she did or your story of what you think she did, you were loved. You are loved. This is the moment you understand you need her guidance. She is establishing standards for you, setting the compass for you, securing safe passage in the world for you *and* the family. She had and has more than your interests at heart. By the time she is ageing and old she has the interests of the whole world at heart.

And yet we know, they will love us when we are dead. They will love us deeply when we are dead. They will love us for the wonder they had a mother and a grandmother. They will love us for the knowing she is in their bones. They will love her for the ache in their heart and the awakening that her living spirit is now their living spirit. For the awe that she is their mind, and she is everywhere. And, like the rest of us, they will be left wondering what was so dreadfully wrong with their mother.

I dream of my grandson. I am lying on the bed. He leans over and kisses me on the cheek. It is a gesture of love from the man who remembered, for a split moment, well below the bitter radar of other people's stories, he remembered he loves his grandmother.

I dream again of my granddaughter. She is a child, exactly as she was, only she is as estranged in the dream as she is in life. As we walk along I put my arm around her shoulders, and she leans into me as once she would have, easy loving except this was the easy need-loving of the estranged granddaughter. As always in these dreams they are a check-in for her. She comes to drink from the well, a vital visit from the soul spirit of one who needs to be reminded and remember she is loved, restored enough to head out again on the lonely road.

As I write these final words, I am tentative about unleashing into the world the ideas I have woven, the words I have written and the meanings I have made. There is no righteous intent here, neither blame nor anger directed towards any individual. If there is any intent it is to invite us all to get forensic about the language and ideas we grasp onto to save us from the pathogenic madness of modern industrialised western living.

It is a call to get geological, drill down through time, past the ad men and the industrialists and beyond reach of the profiteers. Find the oldest sources you can for the meaning you seek. Focus on what is meaningful and whole about your place in the scheme of things. We who have everything owe this to the world that gives us so much.

To the empowered sibling adults at the head of industrialised family units I offer this: Love is a hand reaching. Living asks us to be brave. Let us be braver still and teach the children Loyalty, that they might intimately know the nature of Love.

To the legion of ageing mothers of adults feeling their way along the edges of industrialised nuclear families, I offer the most exalted phrase I have ever heard, from author Chris Cleave: Everything brave is forgiven.

Everything brave is forgiven.

This book is a brave endeavour. To my own adult children and grandchildren, thank you. For the years. For the love. For the laughter. For the tears. For the turning tide of recognition for the omphalos of the motherline.

And finally, to answer the question in the introduction to this book: What is the 'this'?

The 'this' is Love.

These passing days I am no longer admired for my hair or my skin or my youthful looks. I didn't look my age as an adult until the day my mother died, at which point I grew into her skin. Each morning I glance in the mirror and I'm pleased with the aged face that smiles back at me. I wear my mother's skin like a hard-won battle cloak. It is my trophy. My apology. My reverence. My pride. I earned this cloak. I earned this wrinkled skin. I earned this broken heart. My mother in my body is what is left to me. It is my due given it was what was left for my grandmother, and my great grandmother, and my mother. Unpartnered, untethered women, all of us strong brave devoted. Here we stand. All of us, here in my living skin. In two short decades this skin will be my daughter's battle cloak. Isn't that wild? In twenty years, my daughter will look like me now. She will be nearly seventy. The battle cloak will be hers in which to send apologies up and down the family line, and most particularly to a heaven she doesn't believe in.

Here at the omphalos stone in the temple of family life, we meet the ageing mother as more than symbol. She is alive. She is the place where worlds touch. She is a channel. A passage. And she knows how to use this gifted power.

The bequest maternal, the legacy eternal.

# Key References

Adler, A. (1997). *Understanding life.* Oneworld Publications.
(Original work published as The Science of Living in 1927).

Adler, A. (1923). *Understanding human nature.* George Allen &
Unwin.

Antonovsky, A. (1979). *Health, stress and coping.* Jossey-Bass.

Antonovsky, A. (1988). *Unravelling the mystery of health: How people
manage stress and stay well.* Jossey-Bass.

Arendt, H. (2017). *The origins of totalitarianism.* Penguin Classics.
(Original work published in 1951).

Astbury, J. 1996. *Crazy for you: The making of women's madness.*
Oxford University Press.

Bly, R. (1997). *The sibling society.* Knopf Doubleday.

Coffey, J. (2020). Assembling wellbeing: Bodies, affects and the
'conditions of possibility' for wellbeing. *Journal of Youth Studies,*
1–17.

Dahlberg, K. (2007). The enigmatic phenomenon of loneliness.
*International Journal of Qualitative Studies on Health and
Well-being, 2*(4), 195–207.

Dale, S. (2023). *How do adults make sense of a wellbeing-through-
writing program?* [Doctoral dissertation, Queensland University
of Technology.] https://eprints.qut.edu.au/244018/

De Beauvoir, S. (1996). *The coming of age.* WW Norton & Company.
(Original work published in 1971).

Hemberg, J., Eriksson, K., & Nystrom, L. (2017). Love as the original source of strength for life and health. *International Journal of Caring Sciences, 10*(2), 629–636.

Hornstein, G. A. (2000). *To redeem one person is to redeem the world: The life of Frieda Fromm-Reichmann.* Other Press.

Hyde, L. (2019). *The gift: How the creative spirit transforms the world.* Vintage.

Killeen, C. (1998). Loneliness: An epidemic in modern society. *Journal of Advanced Nursing, 28*(4), 762–770.

Kingsley, P. (1999). *In the dark places of wisdom.* The Golden Sufi Centre.

Levine, P. A. (2010). *In an unspoken voice: How the body releases trauma and restores goodness.* North Atlantic Books.

McGraw, J. G. (2000). Longing and the phenomenon of loneliness. In A. Tymieniecka (Ed.) *Life creative mimesis of emotion: From sorrow to elation: Elegiac virtuosity in literature (pp. 33–60). Springer Netherlands.*

Rubin, H. (2007). *The Mona Lisa stratagem.* Grand Central Publishing.

Szasz, T. S. (1961). *The myth of mental illness: Foundations of a theory of personal conduct.* Harper Perennial.

Todres, L., & Galvin, K. (2010). "Dwelling-mobility": An existential theory of well-being. *International Journal of Qualitative Studies on Health and Well-being, 5*(3), 5444.